D1125053

The Coming Influence of
CHINA

Revised and Updated

Carl Lawrence and David Wang
Foreword by C. Peter Wagner

SHANNON
PUBLISHERS

The Coming Influence of China
Revised and Updated
© 2000 by Carl Lawrence and David Wang

Published by Shannon Publishers
PO Box 575
Artesia, CA 90702

Shann Publ@aol.com

Printed in the United States of America

International Standard Book Number 0-9638575-3-3

Dedicated to:

Paul E. Kauffman,
teacher, mentor, missionary to China

CONTENTS

FOREWORD

China is a phenomenon. Hardly a day goes by in which major American newspapers don't have at least one article related to China. "Made in China" is stamped on an enormous number of goods sold in American stores. It is impossible to think of our 21st century world without putting China up toward the top of the agenda.

But what is happening in the secular socio-economic-political world in China takes a back seat for Christians. Why? It is because in recent years in China we have seen with our own eyes the most massive and most rapid evangelistic harvest of souls recorded in all of human history! It could well be that there are now as many born-again Christians in China as there are in the United States.

I'll never forget the day, twenty years ago, when David Wang walked into one of my classes in Fuller Seminary. John Wimber had just joined me in teaching MC510 "Signs, Wonders and Church Growth." This was new to me, so I asked David, "Have you seen any signs and wonders over there in China?" He began talking non-stop!

We at Fuller were amazed at his stories about what God was doing in China. At that time information from China was very limited. However, David Wang of Asian Outreach had been visiting the different provinces of China on a regular basis, and he brought first-hand information about what was happening there. He attributed the phenomenal growth of the church in China to the power of God manifested in so many ways by miracles, signs and wonders.

Since David's graduation, we have kept in touch and have ministered together on many different occasions. When I visited David in Hong Kong, I discovered that what he had shared in my classroom was just the tip of the iceberg. What God is doing in China today is so amazing that it reminds me of the verse in Habakkuk 1:5: *Look among the nations! Observe! Be astonished! Wonder! Because I am doing something in your days—you would not believe if you were told.*

Ten years ago, when speaking to a group of leaders in Hong Kong, I prophesied that by the year 2025 China will be the nation of the world sending out more foreign missionaries to other countries than any other. I now believe even more strongly that this will happen.

To those who have been praying for China, this book will be a tremendous encouragement. Your prayers are being answered!

To those who have been giving to missionary work in China, this book will show you that the seeds you have been planting are bearing much fruit. This is especially true of Asian Outreach. I place them at the top of the list of today's "third-world mission agencies." My policy is not to join ministry boards, but I could not help making Asian Outreach an exception to my rule.

To those who have never given China a second thought, it is my prayer that, as you read this book, you will be aware that God loves the Chinese people and that He is doing a great work among them.

This book tells the story of one of the most exciting moves of God in all of history. As I have heard David Wang say many times: "Look out! The Chinese are coming!"

C. Peter Wagner, Chancellor
Wagner Leadership Institute

INTRODUCTION

There is a vast difference between history and that which is historic. Everything that happens is history, but only that which is significant is historic. What makes an event historical is its "sign" character—it points beyond the event to something greater, usually paralleling previous events, and often repeating itself. That is a fact we sometimes ignore at our own peril.

For example, go back to August 14, 1947. From India's Khyber Pass to Kashmir, from the jungles of Assam to New Delhi's India Gate, quietly, but not unnoticed, an historical event was unfolding. The British Union Jack, which had flown for three centuries from flagstaffs throughout India, was quietly lowered for the last time. Eighteen hours later, hundreds of thousands of people gathered as the hot August sun peaked over New Delhi's Sandstone Arch, a monument dedicated to the 90,000 Indians who died to keep that now absent Union Jack flying. Bleachers set up for dignitaries began to creak and fall, and were soon trampled by the crowd surging forward to see the naked flagstaff. "It is raining babies," the people cried, as women threw their children up in the air so they would not suffocate in the crushing surge of farmers, merchants, beggars, and students.

Soldiers pushed people aside to make way for a Rolls Royce,

its horn beeping, that was slowly making its way to the flagstaff. Soon the crowds had climbed atop the automobile to get a better view of this historical moment. Realizing that he was as close as he was going to get by car, Louis Francis Albert Victor Nicholas Mountbatten, Viscount of Burma, Admiral of the Fleet, Viceroy of all India and personal representative of His Majesty, King George VI, crawled through a partially-opened car door. His white uniform was soon spotted by the sweat of the undulating mass around him. With his medals pushed against his chest, he looked up through the crowd and yelled to the Prime Minister of the new nation, "Nehru, raise the flag!"

Instantly, the crowd was silent. There were no bands, no cannons—they had all been overwhelmed and pushed aside. The Viceroy then lifted his arm above the crowd and gave a stiff salute as, for the first time in history, the flag of the new Republic of India made its way up the staff. When the Viceroy's arm came down it signified for all of history that the greatest jewel in the British Crown was gone from it forever. The hot sun continued its slow descent, a sun that was quickly setting on a great Empire.

Now move ahead five decades, one minute to midnight, June 30, 1997. The Viceroy from India is now dead, victim of an IRA bomb. His favorite nephew, His Royal Highness, the Prince of Wales, heir to the throne of his Empire, sees history repeat itself. In front of Government House in Hong Kong, the Union Jack is lowered from its staff. The last great jewel in a crown of a great Empire is folded away with the flag.

A few blocks away, the invited heads of over 100 nations stand in respect as, for the first time in 100 years, the Premier raises the flag of the People's Republic of China and the Five Stars sway aloft over Hong Kong.

This historic moment is not just a simple, political "turnover" of a piece of real estate. It is a "sign" signaling the near end of one great Empire, and the resurgence of another. It tells the world that the Opium War is over—and one side has won. It sends a message to 1.28 billion people saying we are again a sovereign nation and the *gweilos* (foreign devils) have departed from our shores. True, there is the matter of Taiwan, but prodigal sons return in time.

The parallels between India, 1947, and Hong Kong, 1997, are obvious, but very different. Whereas 1947 bespoke "new democracies" and "shrinking empires," the change of 1997 bespeaks a second "super power" and how the other holder of that most dubious distinction will accept this new fact of life. Though the implications of 1947 caused nary a blip on the world's economic, political and social Richter scale, 1997 registered a silent upheaval and a possibly devastating slippage of a major world fault. That means that the other "super power" (i.e. the United States) can no longer ignore the potential abilities of one-fifth of the world's population. Nor can the United States afford to repeat the previous catastrophic mistake of assuming that "those Asians" can never compete—that all they make are "trinkets and toys." That was an act of arrogance whose aftershock is still leaving many surveying the ruins and wondering why they didn't anticipate that "toys" would now be called "Toy-otas."

Hong Kong is, in effect, the public assertion that China is a major world power that will exercise tremendous influence on the rest of the world, the U.S. included. However, to limit China's influence on America to bankers, entrepreneurs, and generals, is to miss the whole point of history. Hong Kong and 1997 was one of those historic "signs" that light the past, the present and the future.

Hidden beneath the political and commercial veneer is a great truth. It points to the fulfillment of a greater kingdom, one in which all flags of all nations will be lowered to make room for one simple blood-stained banner. China's influence on America as well as the entire Western world will, more than anything else, be spiritual in nature. History, the fine line of time that connects all things historic to past and present, is woven together by many people who are unconsciously fulfilling their role.

Now, go back into history again. It is 1968. The new Middle Kingdom emperor, Mao Zedong, tries to regain control of his revolution. He produces a "Little Red Book" and red armbands, and he calls the youth of his nation to "cleanse the revolution of all foreign influence." They shut down transportation and close factories and schools. The Red Guards become judge and jury. Trials are held in courtyards and on street corners. The intelligentsia and professional people are sent to the countryside for "corrective labor." Schoolteachers are executed by their students.

At Number 27 Macdonnell Road, in Hong Kong, a Chinese kid on the first floor and an American missionary on the fourth floor, in their own separate ways, attempt to pierce a curtain that separates China from the rest of the world. They both see the bodies with hands tied behind their backs, floating down the Pearl River into the Hong Kong harbor. They listen in different locations to answers to the same questions as escaping refugees tell of the carnage ravaging the homeland. Little do they know that as one kingdom is decreasing, another is increasing.

That is what this book is about. It adds sinew, sweat, blood, and tears to Mao's statement, "A revolution is not a dinner party."

REVOLUTION

Section One

1

THE CULTURAL REVOLUTION

"A revolution is not a dinner party."
—Mao Zedong

Just how significant the change in China has been in the last thirty years, since the start of the Cultural Revolution plunged the country into a long nightmare, was recently illustrated in Guangxi Province. Red Guards appeared in Nanking wearing baggy uniforms, Mao badges and red armbands. There was a major difference from thirty years ago, however. The uniforms were costumes and the armbands said "service personnel," instead of Hong Wei Bing. These "Red Guards" were waitresses for a new fast food chain.

Owner Tan Yonghua, Red Guard at age 11 but now turned capitalist entrepreneur, admitted, "Some people get angry when they see the waitresses. They remember how they were persecuted, how the Red Guards killed counterrevolutionaries, sometimes their own teachers."

"Yes," chimed in one middle-aged customer as she dug into her rice and boiled pork, "it's a little strange, but the service is good." Another customer admitted to being a Red Guard himself but said, "That was a historical period and we have to accept that."

For millions of Chinese, the Cultural Revolution was no fast food meal served on stainless steel dishes by smiling waitresses, nor did anyone call it "a little strange" dinner party served by a revolutionary.

Back then, Mao Zedong was losing control of his revolution. The Party was falling apart from one too many of his great movements "forward." The "Old Revolutionary" had voraciously swallowed all the fawning adjectives heaped upon him by the Western press and intelligentsia. Now, the 850 million nouns and pronouns at home needed food and clothing—the basic necessities of life that he had been promising since 1949—but the only provision he had produced was a stark poverty of both body and spirit.

The "Venerable Old Man," his face sagging in spite of makeup, breathed heavily from the tight girdle he wore to hold in his distended stomach, bloated by his traditional eight-course evening meal topped by several glasses of fiery mao tai. He traveled from one of his luxurious apartments to the office of the Central Committee. He helped affix the first wall poster that was to be the symbol of the new great movement: the Great Proletarian Cultural Revolution. The poster called on the young people of China to "bombard the headquarters" of local party leaders. China's millions of youth, teenage students, were given red armbands imprinted with the words, "Hong Wei Bing" (Red Guards). With the armbands came authority to "cleanse the revolution." They were authorized to be judge, jury, and executioners. The Red Guards were now the vanguard of a movement that would bring the world's largest nation to the brink of total chaos and disaster.

With the first wall poster in place, Mao went in the Gate of Heavenly Peace Square, at the center of Beijing, for a "rally of one million" of his executioners. Each was given a little red book called *The Quotations of Mao.* Just as their arm bands were symbols of their authority to "cleanse the revolution forever," the "Little Red Book" held aloft became the symbol of their commitment to nothing less. No one would stand in their way and survive.

The ruthless efficiency of their task was illustrated on a cool autumn day in 1966. In the suburbs of Beijing, an elderly lady sat in her wooden chair, hands folded in her lap. Her faded, loosely fitted, blue tunic hung from her stooped shoulders. She was waiting for the Red Guards, knowing they would come, just as they had for so many others.

She glanced across the small room at her husband and then at the pictures sitting in ornate frames on the top of a chest of drawers. Among them was a degree from a prestigious foreign university, and a marriage certificate. Inside the top drawer, hidden under her miniscule but politically correct wardrobe (two more tunics and three pairs of trousers), was a little money secretly saved for some special occasion. She knew what was about to happen. As tears began to well up in her eyes, she put both elbows on the small, oilcloth-covered kitchen table and placed her head in her hands.

She could not bear to look across the room at the bed where her marriage had been consummated twenty-six years before. Childhood sweethearts had become husband and wife. In this place, three children had been brought into a society that was supposed to get better, but only seemed to get worse. Everything had looked so promising. There was to be no more war, yet their young men went off to Korea. There was to be no more famine, yet there were many days, and sometimes weeks, when all they had to eat was a sliced turnip. She remembered the recurring discomfort of standing in line in the freezing winter for as long as five hours just to buy one tiny piece of meat. She took it home and prepared it as if it were a feast. She told her children she was not hungry and that they must eat her share.

She remembered the officials' promise that there would never be another "100 Flowers Blossom Campaign"—that terrible time when members of the intelligentsia were invited to "speak out" against the leadership, only to find their own voices used against them as witness to their sometimes real, but more often concocted, counterrevolutionary activities. Whether in prison, or left at home to care for the children without food or money, one person after another had to write his or her confession against Mao. It would then be torn up, often without being read, and another, more detailed confession with "all the truths" would be demanded. Eventually, the mind would refuse to cooperate, and one became a naked target for ruthless interrogators.

"You know what he said yesterday?" The woman lifted her head, turning toward her husband's voice. He spoke quietly while looking out the window into the small courtyard that served as a center for the six families living in the enclosure. "It was in the paper, in red ink. 'There is no construction without destruction. Destruction means criticism and repudiation; it means revolution. It involves reasoning things out, which is construction. Put destruction first, and in the process you have construction.

"Imagine that," he stated incredulously as he turned and walked to his wife's side. "Put destruction first, and in the process you have construction. What kind of convoluted reasoning is that?" He hesitated for a moment, then reached over and placed a comforting hand on her shoulder. His long, slender fingers, trained to bring music to a nation so in need of something beautiful, trembled. Without looking, she reached up and stroked the professor's hand with her calloused, knotty fingers.

Suddenly his fingers tightened on her shoulder. Her hand gripped his. They heard it at the same time. The shouting was unmistakable. Their hands trembled involuntarily. The shouting became louder. For several days now, posters had appeared on their front door. One read, "Lover of Foreigners," another "Re-educate these Poisonous Snakes!"

"Maybe they are just passing by." It was a feeble attempt, mingled with hope—a hope that was soon to die. The angry voices grew louder as the crowd entered the courtyard. The professor placed his hands on his wife's arms, then bent over and kissed her on the cheek. He whispered something to her, but it was drowned out by the smashing of the front door. There was a moment of stunned silence as the professor and his wife stared with heartsick disbelief into the face of a former student now standing in front of a crowd that half filled the courtyard. Like 150 million other teenagers, the student wore the prestigious band of the Red Guards on her left arm. Suddenly, as Mao's little red soldiers pushed their way into the room, there was a cacophony of voices shouting: "Parasite!" "Snake!" "Mao has sent us!" "Long live Chairman Mao!" "Capitalist!" "Lover of Foreigners!" The professor and his wife watched helplessly, paralyzed by fear and disbelief as they saw their home being ransacked. She attempted to stand, and cried out in protest as the marriage certificate frame was smashed on the floor. The youth committing the act pushed her back into her chair.

In a few moments it was all over. The "flowers of the revolution," arms full of pictures, books, sheet music, a lifetime of memories and accumulated necessities, carried the confiscated articles into the courtyard and dumped it all in a heap. A young girl walked up to the professor. The room became quiet, as if it was an act that had been repeated often. Without a word, she slapped the professor across the face. With a cry the wife rose to defend him, but a young man roughly pushed her back down on the chair. She wept as she saw the blood coming from the side of her husband's mouth. Before the professor could ask his former student, "Why?" she turned and headed out the door, motioning for the others to follow.

Other youths grabbed the professor and threw him out the door and into the courtyard. The wife, frozen to her chair, placed her hands over her face and wept. Her shoulders heaved as she cried out to an empty room, "Why, why, why?"

Though the Red Guards were not yet as practiced in the art of carnage as they would become, they performed this act of destruction and debasement methodically. First there was the fire, then the sound of flesh being hit by heavy shoes and sticks. Next there was shouting, more kicking and obscenities. Then silence.

Slowly, the wife turned toward the door, which was now hanging on a broken hinge. She stood and gingerly pushed a smashed picture frame aside with her foot. She stepped over the mattress, which had been ripped open to check for more "foreign contraband." The acrid smell of smoke filled her nostrils as she cautiously peered into the courtyard.

The pile of life's treasures and daily necessities was still burning, but the fire was dying. She saw the face of a neighbor cautiously peeking out from the crack of a partially opened door. Then she heard it. It sounded like the moan of a wounded animal.

Following the sound with her eyes, she froze at what she found there. Paralyzed by fear and disbelief, mouth open but unable to make a sound, she stared at the heap of twisted humanity lying on his stomach. He looked more like an animal hit by a truck than her husband. His arms were underneath his chest; one leg stuck out while the other was partially tucked under his body. A cry burst from her throat as she ran to him in the corner of the courtyard and gently knelt beside him. Like a mother reaching out to take her first baby from the midwife, she tenderly turned him over. His eyes were closed; one already swollen shut. Through lips split open, he emitted moans of anguish and pain. As she had done thousands of times before when she wished to comfort him, she reached down and lifted his hands to hold them to her face.

A moment of stunned disbelief, and then she fell across his chest, weeping and holding his two hands to her face. The smell of the burned flesh of fingers held over a fire and the blood from fingertips slashed by razor blades filled her nostrils and smeared her face. Her husband would never again use his long slender fingers, trained by a lifetime of discipline, to bring music to the hearts of their fellow man.

A holocaust known as the Cultural Revolution had begun to stretch its unmerciful tendrils across the world's largest nation. The term "Red Guards" made its entry into the history books, defined by its ignominy and uncontrolled anarchy. However, God's merciful hands would use the Red Guards' seemingly uncontrolled evil for good. We would later find out that God had been writing His own history.

2

MOTHER ZHANG

"I will build my Church."
—Jesus Christ

In late 1968 and early 1969, as the cacophony of the Red Guards began to diminish, another sound rose across the land. This was not the shrill, rehearsed screams of a million parched throats crying out empty slogans. This new sound did not carry the pathos of an innocent person pleading for mercy, nor was it the animal-like moans of the dying. It was not the sound of thousands of running feet pursuing trouble, nor was it the hollow shuffle of feet sent to places they did not want to go. Rather, it was the ordered and measured cadence of an army quietly marching from one battlefield to another—not in defeat, but in victory.

This army was outwardly tattered and torn; its book of instruction had been burned, its meeting halls turned into warehouses or prisons. Young and old, educated and illiterate, united with one purpose. All had been persecuted, horrible violence used against them in attempts to decimate their ranks. Their enemies had used beatings, handcuffs, psychological stress, prison terms at hard labor, and death. They had been shamed in public displays, as "parasites that must be eliminated," like so many "fleas on the back of a dog." They had lost all their human rights. But they could not be stopped. The more they were persecuted, the more

11

they fought. Their weapons were not of this world. After a thousand battles, they moved into a thousand homes, courtyards, fields and caves, to be recharged for the next battle.

They started as 900,000; now they measured in the millions. They were the House Church of China—not just "Christians," but "believers." They did not just profess a faith in Jesus Christ; they were willing to die for it. And hundreds of them did, but millions survived. These were a people who understood that there are casualties in any war. Their Commander-in-Chief had warned them that the day would come when they would be killed and thrown into the streets, and that people would be commended for killing them. Mr. Wang, arrested in March 1958, almost eight years before the beginning of the Cultural Revolution, was one of God's soldiers. He was sent to a labor camp for ten years of "re-education." His crime? He was a professing Christian who refused to deny his faith. In the labor camp, he continued to profess his faith and to witness among his fellow prisoners. He was dealt with very severely, receiving the worst possible job assignments, very little medical care and a minimal supply of food rations. He was placed in a cell with others whose job it was to make him recant his belief in Jesus Christ. His cellmates received extra labor and smaller rations until they could convince the counterrevolutionary to denounce his faith. But he didn't—and they killed him.

A survivor testifies: "Thousands of pastors and devoted believers died because they stood firm in their faith. Additional thousands were sent to prison where they suffered various forms of torture, hard labor and starvation. The government of China gave an edict stating that if anyone was found spreading the 'foreigners' gospel of Christianity, they would be thrown into prison or put to death. Everywhere, believers were watched and much more.

"One of my mother's co-workers, a pastor, was caught by the Communist officials. They tortured and beat him, trying to make him denounce his faith. He would not do it. At last they became so angry with him that they brought a coffin and made him lie in it. They told him, 'All right, now you must make a final decision! Either deny Jesus Christ or we will bury you.' His only reply was, 'I will never deny my Lord.'

"They nailed the coffin shut and left it sitting for a time, listening for a voice from inside. There was none. They screamed and shouted at him and pounded on the casket. Still only the sound of quiet, peaceful breathing. They buried him alive."

Where would this dedicated army meet to get their provisions and orders? Let them tell you: "My home is deep in the mountains of Guangxi where the population is sparse and life is simple. Here we have market days every so often and all the farmers stop work and take their surplus produce to the town fair. They sell rice, peanuts, vegetables, fruit, pigs, chickens and geese, and then they buy household goods. People come and go and the town is extraordinarily busy. They take the opportunity, too, of exchanging news and gossip. But the Christians seize the opportunity to hold meetings.

"During the Cultural Revolution, all the Bibles were burned, the churches were closed and Christians criticized. But the Christians learned how to do battle with Satan and trained themselves, trusting in the Lord. The Christians used to gather at the homes of people like Mother Zhang, taking every opportunity to grow in the Lord and in faith, looking beyond the darkness to the dawn.

"I remember Mother Zhang from when I was a boy. She must have been about 60 then. She became a Christian in 1948 and did housework for a foreign missionary. After the 1949 liberation, because she came from a lower-class background, she got preferential treatment and was sent to work in a children's nursery, but she still remained faithful to the Lord and became highly respected.

"She used to visit all the Christians, who loved to have fellowship with her because she had such a loving heart and was out-and-out for the Lord. If anyone was in trouble, she would come immediately to comfort them and pray. When the clouds of persecution began to gather and the churches in the town came under attack, she quietly prepared herself to be martyred. But God wonderfully led her away into the countryside when the authorities called for dispersion because of the threat of war. Before leaving, she encouraged the brethren from Romans 8: *Who shall separate us from the love of Christ? Shall tribulation? Or persecution?* 'Remember,' she said, 'We are more than conquerors through him who loves us.' When she left, everybody wept.

"Life in the mountain village was hard and lonely, but she prayed without ceasing and kept close fellowship with the Lord, longing to find other Christians. One day, when she went to borrow firewood from a neighbor, she overheard a woman talking to her 8 year old son: 'Who told you that apart from class love there is no other love?'

"'My teacher told me.'

"'No! Listen, son,' the mother said. 'There are many kinds of love. Your parents love you, your sister loves you, and there is a book which says God has an even greater love for people.'

"Mother Zhang then asked her in a low voice, 'Do you have a copy of this book (the Bible)?'

"'Oh, would you like to read it?' the neighbor replied.

"'I already have it myself,' Mother Zhang happily cried.

"From then on, God wonderfully knit them together. Through this neighbor, Mother Zhang got to know three more brothers and two sisters. They hadn't had a meeting for three years, but quietly they began to pray about what to do.

"After some time praying, they all decided to meet at Mother Zhang's home because all in her family were Christians. But they were still concerned about how they could avoid drawing attention to themselves and the inevitable persecution.

"God showed them that they should meet on market days when there were so many people about and the Communist cadres would be too busy to pay attention to the small group.

"Mother Zhang decided to set up a food stall downstairs for the visiting farmers, as there were not enough teahouses in the town. She hadn't had it open a month before it was packed with farmers and she had to increase the number of tables from three to seven.

"All sorts of people came in and she seized the opportunity to share the gospel with them. Meanwhile, upstairs, the Christians could have their meeting safely because of the general hubbub of conversation down below.

"I first attended their meeting in March 1973. Eight other Christians attended. The bread and nine teacups were laid out on a table in preparation for the Lord's Supper. After a sister prayed, Mother Zhang preached on 'The Christian's Life of Prayer.' She wasn't a pastor or an evangelist, had no special formal theological training but she was able to emphasize the importance of prayer from her actual experience and testify to the Lord's faithful promises. 'Prayer,' she said, 'is like a radio antenna. It beams our prayers to God and can also receive His answers.'

"Suddenly her daughter's voice was heard from downstairs with the secret warning that the police were coming: 'Mother, we've run out of salt!' Mother Zhang immediately went out and after a long, heavy silence in the room, returned with her daughter. A false alarm! Quietly everyone hummed a hymn and Mother Zhang gave communion.

"Then I explained how they could listen to gospel programs on the radio and they all burst into tears and praised the Lord. Finally, Mother Zhang gave out the names of the people she had witnessed to, and news of Christians in other places. The whole service lasted for fifty minutes.

"Later, I received a letter from the daughter, saying the church had grown rapidly to twenty-four people. They couldn't meet in one place anymore, and had split into two separate meetings. The new meeting was in a remote mountain village that had six households and had formed its own production brigade. The 40 year old brigade chief had become a Christian only recently. He led four others to the Lord; three were young intellectuals who had been 'sent down to the countryside.'"[1]

Mother Zhang represents only one of thousands who gather together, meeting illegally throughout China.

Notes:

1.   Millions of young people from the cities were sent to do manual labor on the farms. This movement was referred to as being "sent down to the countryside." They were greatly resented by the peasants.

3

PEOPLE
OF GOD

"And the gates of hell shall not prevail against it . . ."
—Jesus Christ

No matter where or when they meet, or under what circumstances, the house church was then and is now made up of one thing: people. Sometimes the absence of those who are not there is as significant as the presence of those who are.

Missing is a young science teacher, a Christian who refused to teach Darwin's theory of evolution as truth. She told the officials that Darwin was anti-God and that the theory of evolution was not true. For weeks they tried to persuade her. Good science teachers were difficult to find; most had been purged and sent to labor in the countryside. She would not relent. Her reply was always the same.

"We are not monkeys. We are men and women made in the image of God." She would later cry the same words through broken teeth and bloody lips.

There is another noticeable void left by a beloved doctor who refused to confess that "Chairman Mao is greater than Christ." He was beaten and left unconscious by the Red Guards. They covered him with a blanket and left him to die on the hospital floor. A few days later they returned and his declaration did not change: "My

Christ is the Lord of Lords and King of Kings. He has been given a name above all names in heaven, on earth, and under the earth."

More beatings followed, but the response remained the same: "Christ is the greatest." After several days, they decided to end this heresy once and for all. They stripped him naked and made him stand up on a narrow bench, barely six inches wide. "Now," they shouted, "if your Christ is bigger than Chairman Mao, let him save you! Our Chairman Mao can save you; just admit it."

Quietly and barely audible, he repeated the story of the men in the fiery furnace. He raised his voice as he looked at his persecutors and told them, "They were not burned because the Lord stood with them, and He is with me now."

The hours passed; not a muscle in his body moved. Five hours . . . ten hours—people began to take notice. "Where does this old man get his strength?" they asked. His very presence was becoming not only a witness to Christ, but also a source of conviction and embarrassment to the others that saw him standing, naked, on the bench.

Finally, the cadre leader could stand it no longer. Naked and without a whimper, the man who believed that "Christ is greater than Chairman Mao" had stood, balancing himself on a narrow bench, from seven in the evening until ten the next morning—fifteen hours of what he called "peace and fellowship." The Red Guards promised him that there would be another day. It came a week later. After dragging him away from his patients, they hanged him.

The Red Guards fought among themselves. They were frightened. Some wanted to cut him down before he died. After a scuffle, one cut the rope. As he fell to the floor, he preached his last message: "As I was hanging there, my heart was melting for you." Then, like his predecessor Stephen, he died.

What about those who do attend house church meetings? What are they like?

Looking across the small room, we see her sitting quietly on a plain wooden bench. Her faded black tunic is a size too big for her, as are her gray, baggy pants. Her eyes are closed. Her shining face, framed by her black, "bowl-cut" hair, presents a picture of serenity that belies the difficult road she has traveled.

She was only nineteen when her crumpled body was roughly thrown into a dungeon cell. There was no light. All she knew was that she was somewhere underground. The floor was wet. The smell told her it was human excrement. Rats and vermin were everywhere. There was no bed or toilet, so if she were to get any rest, it would be while sitting in her own waste and that of others before her. As she sat on the floor she felt something warm run down her arm. She grabbed it and for the first time realized she was still bleeding from the beating.

Her body began to swell from the beating. Silently, squatting so as little of her body as possible would rest on the floor, she began to thank the Lord that she was worthy to suffer for Him. All she would have had to do was denounce her Savior; she refused, and here she was—alone, beaten and weeping tears of joy as her cell became her house of peace. Quietly she asked Him for wisdom and strength—not that she would get out of that terrible place, but that wherever He put her, she could continue to preach the gospel of her Lord.

As the days passed, she became accustomed to the darkness. The bleeding stopped and the swelling went down. As she sat quietly singing a hymn, the Lord gave her a message: "This is to be your ministry."

"But," she objected, "I am all alone. To whom can I preach?" She continued to pray that her ministry would be fulfilled. Suddenly an idea came to her. She stood up and called for the guards.

"Sir, can I do some hard labor for you?"

The guard looked at her with contempt, mingled with surprise. No one had ever made that kind of request of him before.

"Look!" she exclaimed. "This prison is so dirty. There is human waste everywhere. Let me go into the cells and clean up this filthy place. All you will have to do is give me some water and a brush."

Not to her surprise, she soon found herself on her hands and knees cleaning and preaching from cell to cell. She was looking into the faces of people barely recognizable as human beings. Through continuous torture, they had lost all hope of ever seeing another human being who did not come to beat them.

"Oh," she told us, "when they realized that they could have eternal life, they would get so excited. They would fall down on the dirty floor and repent of their sins, and do you know that very soon all the prisoners believed in Jesus Christ?"

When the Communist officials found out what had happened they were furious. They had lost control over their prisoners. When they were yelled at or beaten, they would only say, "We forgive you in the name of Jesus."

Then it was her turn. She was taken from her cell and beaten, then told to write a confession. The warden sent a pile of paper and a pencil and told her to start confessing her sins against the State.

"Lord," she said, "I have done nothing wrong. What shall I write?"

Slowly the words came. Then she wrote faster and faster. She finally finished and with aching fingers, handed the confession to the guards to be delivered to the warden.

Soon the warden called her to his office. He was trembling with rage. How dare she write such anti-revolutionary things! He then read her confession to a large group of people. It was the Lord's plan of salvation for all mankind. As he read, he began to read more slowly and with meaning. Some were greatly moved by this written plan of God's salvation.

At the same meeting, squatting on the floor, is another lady. She looks larger than she really is in her threadbare, traditional gray jacket and blue, baggy pants. Her eyes are closed. Her hands are folded and held to her lips. The look of serenity that she displays was purchased at her own Gethsemane. After considerable prompting, she reluctantly shares her story.

"After several years of teaching, the Communists came and told me that as a teacher, I should not be preaching the gospel. I could have my job only if I would not preach. I would always pray before I ate my food. My cadre leader got very angry with me. He told me that it was superstitious and that I should not pray before I ate. He warned me that if I ever did it again he would have me arrested. I could not help but thank Jesus for supplying my food, so at the next meal, I prayed. The cadre leader had me arrested and I was sentenced to three years in prison for being 'anti-revolutionary.'

"After the three years, I was called in and told, 'Your brain is washed. Do you still believe or not believe in your Christ? Have you thought it clearly through?'

"I could only reply, 'I have already thought it through very clearly. I will still believe in God. I will still pray.'

"I was sentenced to another three years of hard labor.

"After the three years, I was again asked the same question, only this time they were much nicer. 'If you will stop believing in your Lord, we can release you right now—today.'

"It was not a temptation to me. I simply said, 'I still believe in my Lord.'

"They shouted at me, slapped me about and yelled, 'Your mind is incorrigible; you are hopeless! Your mind needs to be washed even more. Three years is not enough. This time we will sentence you to five years.'

"Five years later, I was again brought before the Communist officials. They were very nice as they told me, 'Now we are really deciding to release you. If you only make one statement—that you don't believe anymore—you can walk out of here, free.'

"My answer was the same. 'No, I cannot.' They shouted and yelled, 'You cannot be redeemed!' Again back to prison."

Fifteen years later she was freed, not because she recanted, but because they didn't know what to do with her. Her presence frightened them.

The service begins as a man, standing in the center of the now full room, begins to pray aloud. Others soon join in. They know that this is a brother who has earned the right to lead such a meeting. His testimony still rings in the ears of many present. It is an affirmation to all of the power of the Lord that they have gathered to worship.

"It was 1958. For no reason, I was arrested one day and sent to prison for three years. They could not tell me what crime I had committed because it was not against the constitution of our country to have a religious belief. In 1961, still without knowing why I was in prison, I was sent from one labor camp to another. We would get up before dawn and work with no break, hardly even allowed to go to the toilet. This would continue until eight or nine in the evening. It was dark when we left for work and dark when we returned, but we would often have to gather for another two or three hours of Marxist indoctrination, to 're-educate our thoughts.' Often the temperature was below zero, and we would squat listening to the harangues while shivering, exhausted from the day's work of hauling stones, carrying a hundred pounds of dirt or rock for a distance of ten miles to build roads. Our food consisted mostly of bran and husks, food not fit for pigs.

"Once I was carrying a heavy load on my back and I fainted. As I fell to the ground, my head hit a sharp stone. When I came back to consciousness, all I could think of were my beloved Master's words, 'The foxes have holes, the birds of the air have nests, but the Son of Man has nowhere to lay His head.' I got up, put the load back on my back and carried my burden with renewed strength, telling myself, 'If my Lord suffered so, why should I complain?'

"When the Cultural Revolution took place, I was assigned to a labor camp with 10,000 other forced laborers. I then found out that very few knew why they were there, or what crimes they had committed. It seemed so very hopeless.

"Of the 10,000, only three of us dared to publicly admit that we were believers. The authorities turned them loose to harass and persecute the three of us who dared to stand for Christ.

"The pressure was, indeed, so very intense that not one single moment of the day or night was there any let up. When they walked by us, they would strike us. We always had to go to the end of the food lines and eat what was left. We were isolated, not only physically, but mentally.

"But the worst persecution was when 'friends' would try to reason with us. We knew what they were trying to do. One day a very kind man took me aside and said, "Why do you want to suffer all these things? You have a wife and children. Don't you ever long to go back to them?'

"He could see in my face how badly I wanted to hold my dear wife and children in my arms, and the temptation rose in me as he continued.

"'Once you say you do not believe in God, at once, we will send you back and you can have a big family reunion.'

"This was a terrible temptation for those who wanted to be free and to join one's wife and family.

"I answered, 'But you don't understand. My Lord died for me on the cross. How can I deny Him?'

"I went back to my labor group and the persecution continued. In 1979, things relaxed in China. Thousands of prisoners were released, but not me. I could not understand why. Finally, in 1980, they let me go home."

Not everyone in the house churches is old or even middle-aged. The Three Self Patriotic Movement (TSPM) is the official church in China, and not to be confused with the house church. The provincial TSPM regulations categorically state that it is forbidden to make converts among young people who are underage. It is illegal to convert anyone under eighteen years old, and young people are strongly discouraged from attending religious services.

There is firm evidence that sometimes young people, even those over eighteen, who approach the official churches to be baptized are reported to their work unit. There, pressure is brought upon them to cease attending church. However, despite the intent of the regulations, young people do secretly attend the TSPM churches.

But in home gatherings, young people are always welcome. That is why a young girl of no more than 17 was there. Here is her testimony:

"As they struggled against me, I was getting very depressed and

I asked myself the question, why is this happening to me? I am a good Christian and have never done anything wrong. Why do they struggle against me and not against those who have really done bad things?

"'Do you still believe in Jesus?' they shouted.

"'Yes, yes, I do.'"

By this time, her depression had gone and she no longer felt sorry for herself.

Her tormentors tied a board that was five feet high and twelve inches wide to her back. They plastered posters on the board detailing her alleged crimes. They placed a dunce's cap on her head and gave her a gong to ring so that people would know she was approaching. She was like the lepers of old, crying out, "Unclean! Unclean!" Their mockery continued as they wrote four characters on her hat: "God blesses." They meant it to shame her, but she wore it as a testimony that God, indeed, does bless.

With the tall hat and the gong, she walked up and down the streets, thanking the Lord that she could spread the message that "God blesses."

After they let her go, she returned to her home and in the days that followed many people began to come to her home asking about "the God that blesses."

Across the room is a young man, just a bit older, sitting on the floor, his crutches beside him. Both legs are stretched in front of him. A plastic sandal falls from one of his feet as he raises himself up to reach into his pants pocket. He takes out a small piece of crumpled paper and with both hands gently unfolds it as he settles back onto the hard floor. His lips begin to move as he reads from the scrap of paper. He has brought the Scripture for that night's message. Several months before, he had given his testimony.

"Even though my parents were faithful Christians, I was saved only when I had this accident and became crippled.

"When I was 6 years old, my father, because of his faith, lost his freedom. In my young mind, I can never forget those dreadful moments and experiences. This has deeply wounded my heart and I can never erase it from my memory. What I went through was indescribable. I had to live through my years with the 'black label' that I have a father who was imprisoned in the labor camp.

"I can remember going to the post office to receive a parcel from my father. When the attendant saw where the parcel came from—such and such labor camp—he suddenly produced a different expression. Was it pity, or accusation? I often dreamed of my father. Finally he was released. When I saw him, he seemed to be very different from what I remembered of him when I was a small child. It was ten years since he had been taken to the labor camp. He was young and strong when he left, but he had grown very old.

"Not long after, the Cultural Revolution began. I was 16 and had to leave school to work in the field. It was then that I joined a group of thirty to fifty young people who were simple thinking and created a lot of disorder around the area. We quarreled, drank, stole and were very satisfied with this kind of aimless, carefree life. We did not realize that this was sin because we were living in darkness.

"After the Cultural Revolution, I came to know another group of friends. They were completely different from the last group. They were cultured and civilized. Their leader would often share with us why man was corrupt. I disagreed with him and would not admit that what we were doing was sinful. I even argued with him. I told him that we did this for a reason—to prove ourselves and to revenge those who have caused inequality in our society. Maybe I considered myself quite healthy, strong and courageous.

Yet there has never been a flower that never fades . . . this was my 'golden age.'

"But during an accident I broke my spinal column. From that time on, I have been a cripple, never able to walk again. Actually, when the accident occurred, the doctor predicted that I would not live for more than three months. It has been several years now since that happened and I am still living—praise the Lord! It was then that I learned to trust the Lord and live for Him. Is this not a miracle?

"People may think that I am an unfortunate person. But I don't think so. After this accident, a number of my friends were concerned with my situation, but no one could do anything for me. My temperature was rising each day. One day a friend came to see me. He was a faithful Christian. I had another friend who was visiting me too, but though she came from a Christian home, she was not yet a Christian. Well, this brother told the two of us to join him in prayer for my healing. Quite reluctantly, the three of us prayed together. After praying for thirty minutes, my temperature suddenly went down. This was my first time to experience God's grace, and I felt His healing power in me as I poured out my sins to Him. I experienced and realized that I was regenerated.

"My friends, if I hadn't been so stubborn while I was still healthy, I probably would not be in this state. For in Psalms we learn that a blessed person puts his delight in the law of the Lord, meditating on it day and night, and in all that he does, he prospers. Therefore, my friend, do not let this happen to you before you come to know the Lord. Yet 'even though I walk through the valley of the shadow of death, I will fear no evil, for thou art with me.'"

This is His army—singing, praying, weeping, and worshiping

God.

There is no trace of bitterness; no one speaks of revenge as they answer the question: How did you survive?

"There were times when it was difficult, but that is what it is like to be a Christian here in China. It is a price we are willing to pay," said an old man.

"Tell us about it," we urged.

"I was in one prison where we were inhumanly crowded, with ten prisoners to a tiny cubicle. We were not allowed to speak to each other or doze off during the day. A guard periodically looked into the room through an opening in the door. Many fell ill; others lost their minds.

"One day another prisoner whispered to me, 'We can see that your religious faith really gives you strength.' This was the beginning of my new ministry.

"Another day, a guard burst into the cell and shouted, 'Stop your smiling!' 'I'm not smiling,' I replied. 'Yes, you are!' shouted the guard. When he left, the other prisoners said, 'Your eyes are always smiling and your face glows with joy!' Most of my fellow prisoners were not Christians—that is, not at that time.

"During one period of time, we were sent off to work seventeen hours a day in the rice paddies. We stood in water almost waist high until our bodies were a mass of sores. For a person in his late 50s who was not used to such work, it was nearly unbearable. But even worse was having to listen almost continually to the foul language used by the other co-workers. When I complained to the Lord about it, I felt Him say to me, 'Are you holier than I? I left the absolute purity of heaven to live in your sordid world.'

"Many times the Lord spoke to me—sometimes in most unusual ways. Once, when I was young, I had a dream. I found myself going up a mountain leaning on the arm of a man. I heard the words of the Song of Solomon, 'What is this that cometh out of the wilderness?' I felt myself leaning upon the arm of my beloved Lord. Years later, I was taken to a prison located in the mountains. As I was walking up the mountain, I suddenly realized the scenery was the same as what I had seen in my dream as a young person. God had prepared me for this walk up to the prison on the arm of my beloved Lord.

"At about the same time that I was arrested, many other Christian leaders were thrown into prison. The Scripture that came to me was from Zechariah 13: *Smite the shepherd, that the sheep may be scattered.* I feared that would happen to God's flock of children. Now that I am out of prison, I realize that not only has God preserved His people in the midst of suffering, but He is sending revival to many parts of China. Now I intend to personally visit some of those revival areas. I see that Zechariah 13:9 has been fulfilled: *Refine them as gold is refined, and test them as gold is tested. They will call on my name, and I will answer them; I will say, 'The Lord is my God.'*"

Any time of the day or night, any day of the year, anywhere in China, the House Church meets and prepares for battle.

4

THE HOUSE CHURCH

"Often, the only thing we learn from history is that we have learned nothing from history." —Anonymous

A parallel to the House Church in China can be found by going back 2,000 years in history. While China was being ruled by its fifth dynasty, across uncharted deserts and mountain ranges, Jerusalem was under a cruel Roman rule. There was an official church there also, but it was called the Synagogue. Each was controlled by heavy-handed men. Though these men were not as openly torturous as the Red Guards, they were still slavishly obedient to a monolithic pagan dictator.

In stifling, sparsely-furnished upper rooms, small groups of men and women met in house churches. Luke records it for us in the book of Acts 2:42-47:

And they were continually devoting themselves to the apostles' teaching and to fellowship, to the breaking of bread and to prayer.

And everyone kept feeling a sense of awe; and many wonders and signs were taking place through the apostles.

And all those who had believed were together, and had all things in common;

And they began selling their property and possessions, and were sharing them with all, as anyone might have need.

And day by day continuing with one mind in the temple, and breaking bread from house to house, they were taking their meals together with gladness and sincerity of heart, praising God, and having favor with all the people. And the Lord was adding to their number day by day those who were being saved.

The parallels between Jerusalem and China are as exciting as they are haunting.

A Learning Church

". . . they were continually devoting themselves to the apostles' teaching . . ." (Acts 2:42)

Believers in China are acutely aware that it is not enough to begin well; one must continue each day to "run the good race." Just as the "loud sound from heaven and the trembling of the soul" were followed by a time of special activity in Jerusalem, the believers in China felt that they, too, were part of a very special visitation by the Holy Spirit. Now it is time to go on to maturity.

The fear of falling away from the truth or being caught up in a vortex of false teaching is ever present. The believers in China are acutely aware of their need for solid biblical teaching and they have a huge appetite for the things of God. One young house church leader, with no theological training and whose scriptural knowledge is limited to what he has copied by hand from radio programs, said, "My greatest burden and desire is to personally know more about God's Word so that, not only will I be able to grow, but I can teach others as well."

Those in leadership are not the only ones who have this tremendous desire to absorb the Word of God and learn all there is to learn. That hunger extends to the entire body of believers, as the following report from a house church in rural China indicates:

"Whenever a preacher comes to proclaim the Word of God,

Christians gather from miles around. Even when an itinerant evangelist has preached to the point of exhaustion, they are unwilling to let him rest, but urge him to continue expounding the Word. In some cases, they have been known to take hold of his luggage and press him to stay a few more days—such is their eagerness to be taught.

"In this situation, where people have been hungering for the truth for a long period of time, it is essential that the preaching concentrate on the Lord Jesus Christ Himself, the very center! Christians often urge the preacher to help them to come to know the Lord better.

"A preacher was invited to a small town to hold meetings. At dawn, the building was crammed with 600 people, with others packed into the courtyard outside. They were willing to suffer the extremely cold weather in order to hear the Lord's message. Before the preacher arrived, they sang hymns to prepare their hearts to receive the Word of God.

"The preacher spoke five times and the Christians stood and listened from early morning until late at night. Still they did not want to disperse and plucked his sleeve, saying, 'We have never heard such good preaching.' They were extraordinarily eager to hear Bible truth expounded and to have the Lord Jesus Christ set forth clearly to them."

One itinerant preacher told of arriving at a house church to preach. The people anxiously asked him what he was going to speak on. His subject was to be about Jesus Christ in the book of Matthew.

"Oh," they replied, "he is going to preach the book of Matthew. The entire book is about Jesus Christ." They held him to his word. Thirty-seven hours later he finished a verse-by-verse exposition on the life of Jesus Christ as recorded in the book of Matthew.

A learning church needs more than teachers, evangelists and preachers. It also needs the Word from which to preach; it needs Bibles. Though it is taken for granted in many parts of the world, a complete Bible is considered a pearl of great price in the Chinese Christian community.

In 1966, the Red Guards made a concentrated effort to burn all Bibles, hymnals and other Christian literature. They did their job well. Today, it is still not uncommon to see a group of several hundred people with only one or two Bibles.

One lady who has a complete Old and New Testament brings it to the meeting wrapped in linen. When the pastor reads the Scriptures, he gently takes the Bible from the lady, carefully unwraps it and reads the text. When he is finished reading, he hands the Bible back to her. She re-wraps it in the linen cloth, as carefully as others had wrapped the Lord's physical body in linen.

In some house churches, certain people are told in advance what Scriptures will be needed for the next meeting. Each of them will copy one portion and bring it to the meeting. When the leader wants to read or speak from the Scriptures, he collects the handwritten copies and puts them together so he will have the complete text. This way, if police interrupt the meeting, the Bible will not be lost. The most they could lose would be a few handwritten verses.

Other stories tell of the importance believers place on possessing God's Word, and what risks they take in order to distribute it to fellow believers.

"One time fourteen young people were delivering 1,000 New Testaments to a certain village. They were caught by the authorities. The Bibles were confiscated along with the bicycles they were riding. All fourteen were imprisoned for anti-revolutionary activity, which is a capital offense."

Another reports, "I know of one village where there are 5,000 believers and four preachers, but not one complete Bible. One person has a New Testament which begins with the thirteenth chapter of Mark and goes through the book of Titus.

"Two believers from the North heard that there were some Bibles available in the southern part of the country. They saved up half a year's pay so that they could travel to the South and purchase at least one Bible for their fellow believers to study.

"They fasted and prayed on the four-day journey, asking not only for traveling mercies, but that there would be at least one Bible available when they arrived.

"When they reached their destination, they were greeted with the tragic news that there were no Bibles left. The two brothers began to weep at the sad news. The next day, another who had been trusted to safeguard and deliver thirty Bibles heard of their plight and gave them all thirty Bibles. Their weeping was turned to joy as they received their precious gift. They were offered food and rest by their fellow believers, but they refused, saying that they fasted and prayed for the Bibles and they would continue to fast and pray in praise for receiving them as they made their way back home."

Another testified: "When we have financial problems and then receive money from brothers and sisters abroad, we bow our heads to worship God and give Him the glory. This financial help brings great strength to the house church. Yet the greatest help of all is a Bible. Before, when I wanted to read the Bible, I had to travel more than one hundred miles. I would borrow the precious book for only a short time and then I had to return it. One day someone gave our fellowship a Bible. When it was brought into the meeting, we found that we could not talk. Tears were running down our faces. There were shouts of prayer and praise. We handled the Bible with such loving care, thanking God."

Another believer states: "Because of the coming of this spiritual food, members of the body here have received great comfort. In their prayers they have shed tears of thanksgiving. We have also offered much thanksgiving to God for your loving concern for us, and we are asking the Lord to abundantly bless the fruit which you have borne for the Lord, so that you might receive a reward incorruptible and imperishable. For you have brought us sweet spring water at a time when we were in dire thirst. You have become the Lord's messenger of light to us and a warm spring breeze to our hearts."

Those who live in a society where the Bible is available to all may have a hard time realizing the importance of God's Word in the life of a Christian in China.

This letter explains that importance: "Dear friends, praise the Lord! Today I am touched by the Lord's Spirit to answer a few questions. I want to tell you how I feel after I received this Bible. I think the heavenly Father really loves me. I am deeply moved and encouraged; for you, because of His love, are willing to help us in spite of the risk of losing your life. At first, I was challenged and revived. Later, I found the way in this Bible and I came to understand many truths. I also see the will of God. Oh! I only know now that I was a seedling without the watering of rain. Now I am like a thirsty and starving man who sees water and food.

"That Bible helped me a lot after I obtained it. I found the way, the goal, and the truth of life in it, which teaches us neither to follow false teaching nor to walk the wrong road. Before, I had walked on many crooked roads. I depended on my own knowledge and wisdom, which didn't work. Oh, I really thank the Lord. He really loves me. Today, He provided this Bible through you to help me turn to the right road from the wrong one.

"I have more strength after I obtained this Bible. No person will be cheated from now on, for we have the correct way to follow. Many brothers and sisters have turned from the wrong to the right.

"When I received this Bible, many brethren wanted to have one also. I am not the only one who was greatly helped by this Bible; at least 5,000 others were benefited. During the times before I had this Bible, I had nothing to do at home after work. I read fiction or chatted with my brothers and sisters. Since I have the Bible, I don't chat with them anymore. I read my Bible to them as soon as I arrive home. Our spiritual life grows daily and the Lord is pleased more and more.

"Brothers and sisters, I want to tell you one thing. Since I obtained this Bible, tens of thousands of Christians are hoping that they can have a copy of their own someday so that they can read it any time without waiting for a borrowed copy. Now they can't read the Bible any time they want. They all said that if they had a copy of their own, they would read it either at night or in the morning, for there is bread of life in the Bible. Though freedom of religion and Bibles are said to be available in China, in fact we can't enjoy them. At this time, there are tens of thousands of Christians in our province alone, and many are praying with tears about this matter.

"Now that I have this Bible, we can make many things clear. People who cried and shouted before have stopped doing that already. Some who were stubborn before have come to understand and to seek the Lord's will. There were many fake ministers before; now we are able to point them out. There were also many false elders, false teachers and false prophets. The Lord does not forsake us. He opens our eyes and causes us to understand."

A Praying Church

"And they were continually devoting themselves . . . to prayer." (Acts 2:42)

William Barclay, commenting on the characteristics of the early Christian Church, says: "Acts 2:42 tells us that not only did they (the first house church) persevere in listening to the apostles' teaching; they also persevered in prayer. These early Christians had a difficult time. They incurred the hatred and the dislike of pagans and were often persecuted. They knew, though, that they could not face all this without the help which God could give them. They were a praying church."[1]

This describes the House Church in China today. One researcher studying the growth of the house church confirms this. He says: "It appears that the distinguishing feature of the present-day church growth in China is the disciplined prayer life of every believer. Chinese Christians pray to the Lord for (1) a watchful and praying spirit; (2) a burden to pray for others; (3) a time and place to pray; (4) energy to pray with fellow workers; and (5) the right words to use in prayer. In this manner they wish to be a trumpet to call all people to more prayer." Chinese Christians have a motto: "Little prayer, little power; no prayer, no power."

Also important is how their prayer life reaches around the world. Every Saturday morning, in one of China's most important cities, a group of people meets for a day of prayer and fasting. They begin at nine o'clock in the morning and pray until three o'clock in the afternoon, or later than that if need be. They do not talk about prayer; they pray—all day. One day, the "number one" prayer request brought before them was that the "Bible schools and seminaries in the West would remain true to teach only the true Word of God."

This is a group of believers whose leadership has spent an average of seventeen years in prison. Many have only a few slips of handwritten scripture and no hymnals. They meet under the threat of being labeled as anti-revolutionaries. Many have lost their loved ones. Their homes are unheated in the winter and uncooled in the summer. They come together to pray. What do they pray for? Listen to this prayer from a house church meeting:

"Lord! Revive Thy Church! We love to sing this hymn. That is the cry of our hearts. But before the church is revived, I must ask the Lord to revive me. If every Chinese believer is humbly willing to be set on fire by the Lord, then the gospel will spread throughout the land and shine upon the millions of souls in darkness. The spread of the gospel is every believer's responsibility.

"May the Lord grant me the gift of steadfast love to proclaim His love in all its depths. May I have power and authority to proclaim His love perfectly so that the hearers will be convicted or encouraged to follow the Lord with greater zeal.

"May the Lord enable me, when lifting up the cross in proclaiming the message of salvation, to have spiritual wisdom to expound the gospel clearly and fully. When lifting up the cross, to explain the doctrine of the cross clearly and to preach its wonders to move men. Oh, for the gift of raising high the cross! Oh, for the power of the Holy Spirit when preaching the cross! Oh, for the power of the Holy Spirit when preaching the cross, that all men may be drawn to the Lord by the power of the cross!

"May the Lord give preaching ability to expose sin, to make men fear. And the help of the spirit that men may be convicted of sin, of righteousness, and of judgment, and thus earnestly repent.

"May the Lord continually place a spirit of awe in my heart, so that I may obtain humility, and also grow daily in wisdom and knowledge.

"May the Lord grant me by His grace the ability of obeying His Holy Spirit so that I can strengthen my brethren.

"For the gift of expounding the Scriptures by the Scriptures, thus rightly dividing the Word of Truth.

"For the gift of establishing and pastoring the church and for prophetic preaching. For the fullness of the Spirit.

"May the Lord help me to have a time full of life with Him in the early morning.

"For a life that will be a witness, bearing more of the fruit of the Spirit.

"For more successful training in love, faith, patience and reverence.

"For the gift of comforting people.

"For a willingness to suffer.

"For a gentle, humble, sympathetic, unselfish and honest heart.

"May the Lord control my tongue to speak words that will build up others.

"May the Lord enable me to hate pride, jealousy, robbing God of His glory, all sexual impurity, and lying; and to love truth, humility, gentleness, honesty, holiness, self-control, faithfulness, righteousness, goodness, lovingkindness and mercy.

"May the Lord enable me not to love the world or its empty glory, but to be bold and completely committed to God.

"May I have the gift of praising God and of singing spiritual songs.

"Well, I could add more; however, to become such a man is the work of God's grace. If God does not help, man can do nothing.

"In everything we need the Lord, for without Him we can do nothing. If Christ is most precious to us, having Him we have everything. May God be with us, dwell with us and go with us. May God enable you not to lose courage, but to fulfill His will.

May He increase our mutual love, fellowship and encouragement! Emmanuel!"[2]

A Miracle-Working Church

". . . and many wonders and signs were taking place . . ." (Acts 2:43)

To ask a participant in the house church in China whether or not he is experiencing things that might be classified as unusual for believers is to invite a quizzical reply: "I don't know what you mean by 'unusual.'"

"Well, you know . . . things a little strange . . . things that don't happen every day."

"You mean miracles?"

"Yes . . . yes, I guess that is what I mean. Yes, that's what I mean . . . miracles."

"You mean healings?"

"Yes, healings . . . you know, like Mr. Huang."

Mr. Huang was a worshiper of Buddha. His health began to deteriorate until he could not keep any food in his stomach at all. After a thorough examination, the doctor diagnosed his case: "You have a cancer of the liver and are at the terminal stage. There is nothing we can do for you."

Mr. Huang then returned to a small town near his native village to await the inevitable. While there, he heard about a doctor in the town and decided to get a second opinion, or perhaps obtain some medicine that could prolong his life. This doctor was a Christian. Later, this doctor would accompany Mr. Huang as he gave his testimony. The Christian doctor confirmed the first diagnosis as cancer of the liver in an incurable, terminal stage.

The Christian doctor told the man that there was no medicine that could prolong his life, but that if the man would believe in Jesus Christ, he could have eternal life. He carefully explained the gospel to the man and urged him to believe on the Lord Jesus Christ. The doctor also explained that Jesus was the Lord and had the power to heal any sickness if it was His will. "But whether Jesus heals you or not is not important," the doctor said. "What is important is that you have eternal life."

"I want to believe in Jesus," Mr. Huang said. The doctor called in another Christian man, and the three of them knelt in his office as Mr. Huang became a new person in Jesus Christ.

Returning to his home, he told his wife of his faith in Jesus Christ and asked her to remove all the idols from the house and burn them. She did as she was told. She knew her husband's condition was hopeless. From then on, Mr. Huang's condition deteriorated rapidly. Every night, he and his wife knelt and prayed together. He thanked the Lord that no matter what happened to him physically, he now had eternal life. He was gripped by terrible pain. His wife fixed some herbal and chicken soup, but it only made matters worse. In fact, over the next weeks, he became so weak that the family began preparations for his funeral. The coffin was purchased and the grave dug on the hillside.

One night a man in a white robe appeared to him in his sleep. The man was holding a knife. Not knowing what he intended to do, Mr. Huang struggled with the man in white, but the man prevailed and touched Mr. Huang with the knife. He awoke the next morning at 8 o'clock and was hungry for the first time in many days. After eating a nourishing bowl of egg-drop soup, he fell asleep. When he awakened, he saw two men in white robes standing by his bed. "You have been healed," they said. He reached down and found all the pain and swelling gone. Being extremely hungry, he ate a hearty meal. When his brother came to pay him a last visit, he was amazed to see him standing up and strong. Mr. Huang told his brother that Jesus had touched him during the night and he was completely healed.

This event can be attested to by several of his co-workers and a Christian medical doctor who has witnessed patients being divinely healed.

The miracles that are common in the house church in China are varied. All, however, are for the glory of the Lord. All the attendant benefits, such as giving comfort to the grieving, are also present.

A grandmother took her young grandson, who was in her care, to the rice field to work with her. There was an accident and he was killed. The grandmother was very distraught; she buried him there as best she could, to protect the body from the elements. Then she went to tell the mother and father. The family gathered in the home, grief-stricken at their terrible loss. Suddenly the door opened, and there stood the young son. His explanation was simple: "A man with a white robe came and took me by the hand, lifted me out of the ground and told me, 'Go home. Your mother and father need you.'"

Another incident concerned an old couple who were very dependent on each other. Though they had been Christians for some time, they had no real assurance of what would happen after death. The generations of ancestral worship were hard to forget. One day the husband suddenly died. The wife was distraught, not knowing whether her beloved husband was truly in heaven, or in some state of punishment. She wondered if she would ever see him again.

In the evening, two cadre leaders went to pay their respects to the remains of the old cobbler. As they were standing there, two men in white robes came and lifted the soul of the man—seen in an image—from the casket. As he was leaving on the arms of the two white-robed men, the old man turned to the cadre leaders and said, "Go tell my wife I am going to be with Jesus and I will wait for her."

The comfort that this brought to the grieving wife was added to by the conversion of the cadre leaders.

Some of the miracles are very practical.

A man sent to prison for his religious beliefs had four children—ages 4,8,10 and 12. His wife was made to walk the streets with a dunce cap and the children were treated badly because their father was a "bad element." The problem was that they had no livelihood, and therefore, no food. At the back of their little house was a small pond. No one had ever fished there, but the children made a net and started fishing. They caught enough fish to feed the family. The supply began to multiply. As time went on, they got enough fish not only for their own needs, but enough to trade for other necessities of life. Thirteen years later, the father returned from prison. There were no fish in the little pond from that day on; they were no longer needed.

There are also those miracles that serve as potent testimonies to the power of God to unbelievers.

A 70 year old lady was the only one who had knowledge of most of the daily operations of her family, as well as the operations of a house church. She alone knew where the Bibles were, who the messengers were, who could or could not be trusted. Suddenly one day, she died of a heart attack.

Her family felt lost. She had not been able to pass on the information that was so vital to all. They began to pray, "Lord, restore our mother back to life." After being dead two days, she came back to life. She scolded her family for calling her back. They reasoned with her. They said they would pray that in two days she could return to the Lord. It would take that much time to set the matters straight.

After two days, the family and friends began to sing hymns and pray that the Lord would take her back. The mother's final words were, "They're coming. Two angels are coming."

This incident caused the entire village to repent.

A Praising Church

"Praising God . . ." (Acts 2:47)

Read this testimony from a meeting:

"What a wonderful, loving Almighty Lord! Jehovah's name is worth praising. His faithfulness goes on for generations. I see with my own eyes that His love lasts forever and ever. As a mother will not forget her infant who needs milk, so much more our heavenly Father will not forget us. Though I have known God since I was young, the pity was that I very seldom had opportunity to read the Word of God. It was like I was blind and could not understand the truth of life. I knelt before God and prayed to Him daily.

"He is truly a God who answers prayers, for things which are impossible for man are possible for Him. While I was thirsting and longing, God provided us the precious Bible through His loving children last year. God's grace should be greatly thanked. Hallelujah! Praise the Lord! From that day on, I studied the Bible every day, and I am enlightened with the truth from the Bible. Countless thanks to the grace of God! Through the teaching of the Bible and earnest prayer, many young brothers and sisters understand that there is eternal life in the Bible.

"Praise the Lord! There is this brother who was put into prison. He refused to stop lifting his hands up in praising the Lord, so he was put into chains and handcuffs along with leg fetters. His flesh was slowly being rubbed off until the bones of his feet were showing. Still he kept lifting up the name of the Lord. He secretly asked an elder brother, 'When there is a change of guard will you baptize me?' It was done while the guards and everyone else were sleeping."

Such incidents do not happen only in prison. There are also those who praise the Lord on their way to prison.

"There was this cart full of prisoners being driven to prison. The people on the street could not see the people inside, but they thought they were awful criminals to be dragged away like animals. The authorities did not want us to see them. 'Are they really that sinful?' we asked. Then we found out the truth. These were Christians on their way to jail. They were all handcuffed together and they were happy. There was no dissatisfaction or resentment on their faces. We could hear them singing as they went by, 'Lord, you are worthy to receive praise. Praise the Lord.'"

An Accepted Church

"*. . . having favor with all the people . . .*" *(Acts 2:47)*

One thing about the first house churches in Jerusalem that caused great consternation among the ranks of the established religious bureaucracy was the respect that the community had for them. The same is true of China's House Church today.

The key to holding many of the house church meetings is the individual cadre leader. Without this leader's permission there can be no meeting. Why do they permit the Christians to come together at all?

One leader answered that question for us. When his superiors asked him why he let Christians hold their religious meetings he replied, "They are good people—very moral and very hard workers. They never give us any problems."

A leader's advancement up the party ranks, or even the keeping of his present job, is most often dependent on meeting production goals. What applies to the local leader reflects upward to his superior. Because the Christians are "good, hard workers," the cadres are more successful. This is a chain of events that the cadre leader does not want to break.

Toward the end of the Cultural Revolution, a group of visitors from Hong Kong was taken to a model People's Commune in central China. The local Communist Party Secretary was proud of the outstanding productivity of his commune and that it was now a showpiece to international visitors.

He told his guests that among the many working units in his commune, the one that had recorded the highest yield and the least accidents or problems was the one nicknamed by others as the "Jesus Brigade." "They were sent down to us from different cities as forced laborers for re-education purposes. They were not peasants or farmers before, but they soon became the best working unit. They are always willing to take on the most difficult tasks. They don't fight among themselves. They never steal things from the commune and they don't break any rules." The cadre leader was not against their going around with their nickname instead of being called Work Unit 517. "I told them they can sing their songs during their work," he said.

In a coastal city where the Church of Jesus has literally exploded in the past ten years, the mayor told a visitor that he himself was not a Christian, "but we are no longer fighting against people who believe in their Jesus. Before the Liberation we all knew that in China, one more Christian meant one less Chinese. But today in our city, one more Christian means one better Chinese." There are 2,400 gathering points of Christians in that province alone.

Professor Zhu, who had studied in America from 1984 to 1987, said he began attending church while he was a houseguest in an American professor's home one summer: "They took me in as a family member and their kindness touched me deeply. When they explained to me that they were Christians and it was their God that had changed them, I was open to learning more of that God." He returned to China as a "quiet" believer.

When we visited him on his campus, he told us of his recent conversation with the party secretary of the university. "He first asked me of the changes he noticed in me. He said I was so much more happy and at peace with myself. I told him America made me more knowledgeable as a professor, but Jesus had made me more 'abundant' as a human being. The party secretary was very interested and accepted from me a copy of the testimonial booklet, *The Story of a Scientist.*"

It is now no longer a secret in China that many Communist Party members are becoming believers of Jesus Christ.

A Mission-Minded Church

They ". . . went about preaching the word . . . " (Acts 8:4)

From that upper room, those first disciples spread the fire of the Gospel of Jesus Christ across the world. This same thing is happening in China.

There seem to be as many ways of witnessing in China as there are believers.

For example, an older woman in a major city has tracts sent in from outside the country. Several days a week, she takes those tracts and a pair of glasses that make her appear farsighted. She climbs aboard a bus, puts her glasses on, and holds the tracts at arm's length from her eyes. Others, as they always do in China, begin to read the tract with her. When she senses that someone is very interested and could accept the tract without too much problem, she simply says, "Do you understand what you are reading?"

Before the person answers, she thrusts the tract in his hand, gets off the bus, and waits for the next one to come along.

Her mission field is a bus. Her place of ministry changes every few blocks, but her message remains the same.

The House Church is interested in reaching those far outside its own community as well.

While visiting China in 1983, we experienced first hand what was known as the "anti-crime campaign." In actuality, it was a move by the government to get "volunteer laborers" to move to the western frontier to help drill oil wells. This is probably some of the roughest country in the world. Those "volunteers" knew that not many returned from the frontier.

Because there were no volunteers, the government issued a decree that every town would register all its criminals. In effect, what they were saying was that almost everyone had to register. Nearly everyone had already been forced to write a confession. Those confessions were considered unacceptable unless they confessed to crimes against the State—real or imagined. Some confessed that they had stolen bottles of ink at school; that would be a crime against the people. Others confessed to forging ration cards or some other crime that would usually have gone unnoticed. Now, those crimes were brought to light.

A pyramid chart of criminals was required of every town; the worst criminals were placed at the peak of the pyramid. The other "criminals" were listed below in descending order, according to the seriousness of the crime. In some villages, where there was little real crime, the most innocuous "act against the people and the state" could send its confessor to the top of the pyramid. Those in that unfortunate position were sentenced to death; the rest of those in the pyramid went west as "volunteer laborers."

As we passed through one small town, we saw villagers being

ordered to stand along the side of the road. Silence permeated the atmosphere of doom. We saw a flatbed truck drive by. Three male prisoners were standing in it—one young, one middle-aged and an older man. They were guarded by soldiers. The prisoners had ropes around their heads to pull their heads up so the villagers could see their faces. Attached above their heads were small plaque-like boards, listing their crimes.

They were then driven to the town square. Although we would have been allowed to view the execution, we walked away. The townsmen watched as a policeman made each prisoner kneel. He walked up to each and shot the prisoner in the back of the head. The families of the "criminals" were then charged approximately ten cents for the bullets used because "the people should not have to pay to do away with these parasites." The rest of the prisoners on the pyramid were sent to the Western frontier, most of whom would never return.

Two young men, 17 and 19 years old, should have been the pride of the Cultural Revolution—as "red" as the sun. Instead, they were followers of Jesus Christ, and they had a special burden to go to the western frontier as missionaries. In a Chinese village, especially during the 1980s when the church was still underground, one didn't go to the Party leaders and say, "I want to go to the frontier as a missionary!" The two young men knew there was one sure way to be sent: they purposely committed a crime. They took the cadre leader's radio and walked down the street with it. They were immediately arrested. They, of course, took the chance that their crime could place them at the top of the pyramid. But it didn't. They were sent to the frontier, where there would be no prayer cards and no furloughs. People in their village have a 24-hour-a-day prayer chain for those two men, who would now be in their early 30s. The church made a covenant with the Lord: they would pray for the two men around the clock until the Lord says, "You can stop now; I've taken them home." They are, the last we heard, still praying.

Another example of the Church's missionary zeal and passion for witnessing can be seen in the life of a man with a wife and two sons. He was arrested by the Red Guards and sent to prison for worshipping a foreign God. Daily, they stripped him naked and balanced a sign from his back and neck that protruded two feet above his head. "Parasite" was written on the front of the sign, and "Worshiper of a Foreign Religion" was written on the back. He was marched down the streets of the neighboring villages. Children were encouraged to throw stones and garbage at him. He was spit upon by some and ignored by others. Dogs followed him, devouring the garbage that fell from his desecrated body.

His nights were spent in a cell too small for him to lie down. He was not allowed to speak unless spoken to.

The warden told him, after one of his regular beatings, "You will die here. I will watch you die. You will never leave this place alive."

Twenty years passed. The people in the village grew bored of the sight of him, so he spent most of his time confined to his small cell. He silently sang to himself. He later verified what other pastors have said, that singing hymns of God and repeating His Word back to Him was what kept them from denouncing his Lord or from committing suicide.

One day he heard the guards talking about someone who was very sick and would soon die. "The warden is right," he thought, "I will die here." Squatting in his "closet," silently repeating God's Word back to Him, he wondered if he even had a voice to sing any more. Words of a hymn ran through his mind, "And He walks with me, and He talks with me, and He tells me I am His own. And the joy we share as we tarry there, none other has ever known . . ."

Unspoken words of praise and thanksgiving filled his heart when suddenly the cell door opened. Two guards shouted at him, "Get out, old man, get out. The warden is dead and we do not want you here. Get out." They pulled his emaciated body from his cell and pushed him toward a door. He heard the cell door slam behind him and the sound of the guards walking away.

For the first time in twenty years, he walked through the prison door unshackled—free.

He looked up at the sky; it was still blue. He had not seen it for months. He took a deep breath of fresh air, opened his mouth and spoke aloud. People walking by quickly turned their heads away and picked up their pace, not wanting to be contaminated by contact with him.

"I don't even know what part of China I'm in," he thought. "I have no money and only these rags to cover my body. Which way is home? Where is home? I have no address."

Across the road he noticed an old woman sitting on the curb with a basket of cigarettes on her lap. With his eyes on her he said aloud, "Lord, it has been twenty years since I have witnessed for you. I wonder if I still know how."

He slowly approached the woman and sat down beside her.

"Cigarettes?" she asked.

A short time later, a passer-by stopped to stare as she made a bonfire out of her box of cigarettes. Yes, he had remembered how to witness, and his testimony was used to bring forth a new creature in Christ—and to set a fire!

The unanswered question in the minds of many is this: Would China still be a vibrant New Testament church without the Cultural Revolution and its persecution? Would there be a Jewish nation without the holocaust? Is the Church nurtured by the blood of martyrs?

Perhaps it's best to leave those questions unanswered and move on to an area in which one does not have to speculate. The Church in China is "a prairie fire out of control." Missiologists and church growth experts acknowledge that what is happening in China is actually surpassing the growth recorded in the book of Acts.

Time might then be well spent reviewing exactly what has happened and what lessons we can learn. We can see how we might be a part of the new wave of God's Holy Spirit, warming our own hands and hearts on His fire. Some people are content to feel the warmth and trust the thermostat; others want to visit the furnace room for themselves.

Notes:

1. William Barclay, *God's Young Church* (Edinburgh: St. Andrew Press, 1970), pp.17-18
2. This prayer was written by the person who gave it in China, and sent by private couriers to Hong Kong where it was translated.

5

TWO EXPLOSIONS

"Suddenly there came from heaven a noise like a violent, rushing wind." —Luke

The growth of the Church in China can be described as two explosions.

The first explosion ignited soon after the 1976 death of Chairman Mao, which resulted in the fall of his Gang of Four and the end of the catastrophic Cultural Revolution. The explosion spread primarily in the rural areas. The house churches there were as bamboo shoots after the spring rain—growth happens everywhere at once and is so fast that it is unstoppable.

Like a wild fire on China's western frontier, Christianity, in its simplest and most unstructured form, spread even into China's most remote provinces. The single spark that started this prairie fire were signs, wonders and miracles. A report from the conservative Lutheran China Study Center on Tao Fung Shan, Hong Kong, concludes that eighty to ninety percent of Christians in rural China are the result of a miracle of healing, casting out of evil spirits, or divine intervention, and of first-hand witnesses' testimonies.

It is worth noting that the believers saw the miraculous as the natural moving of the Holy Spirit. There were no denominational parameters. If a miracle was needed, they prayed for one and it happened. If evil spirits were hindering the fire of the Holy Spirit, they were cast out in Jesus' name. The believers did not separate themselves into bodies of specialists. They did not have to wait for a healing or revival meeting for people to get saved or healed. The small body of believers, not knowing to expect anything less, became the vehicles through which the Holy Spirit worked. There were no labels, only a firm belief that these things were the norm for Christians. They saw that not all were saved and that not all were healed, but they knew that was the business of the Holy Spirit. They simply moved forward as He moved.

It is impossible to know how accurate the report is that 20,000 come to Christ every day in rural China. Most people who have ministered there, however, can bear witness that it is a most unusual phenomenon. Hundreds, and sometimes thousands of sheep gather, looking for a shepherd!

As revival fires from the first explosion burned throughout the countryside, the charge was laid for the second explosion. The more educated and youthful populaces of the cities became increasingly disillusioned with the Communist Party. They had not been fervid worshippers of the deified Mao from the beginning, and especially now that he was dead, their commitment waned. With the collapse of the Gang of Four, an immediate death sentence passed on the Cultural Revolution. The urbanites, who had joined out of fanaticism, slipped away into skepticism, sucked into a spiritual vacuum. This confidence crisis of major proportions shook China's leadership. Before the leaders could respond, the "socialist market economy," Teng-style, hit China. City populations were broadsided by spiraling inflation, sudden unemployment, the ugliest materialism, crude greed, widespread corruption and moral decay. The people witnessed first-hand the demise of Communism as a viable ideology, and they saw the Party hanging on by its fingernails, so to speak, to the claim of mandated absolute ruler.

Desperately, the younger and more learned populace searched in every direction for an alternative. They vented their frustration through underground pop songs with daring lyrics like: "Black was black/Black is now white/Nothing has changed/But the ones who stand on Tiananmen's Gates."

After the violent crackdown on the pro-democracy movement in Beijing's Tiananmen Square, the move to Christianity in major cities of China was so forceful that Party officials repeatedly admonished that Communists are atheists, that they must not join a religious body.

This second explosion reverberated among intellectuals, professionals, enterprising movers and shakers, and even among government officials and their children (many of whom have been educated in the West). This explosion was more subdued but just as pervasive as the first.

Many of these converts have become part of the registered church, the Three Self Movement—many of which are thoroughly evangelical themselves. Where the registered church is not evangelical, believers have slowly migrated to the house churches.

Secret believers, preferring to be called "private Christians," represent a major danger to the present hierarchy because they often hold responsible positions in both the government and the newly controlled economy. The government fears that their influence could parallel that which destroyed Marxism in Europe. They equate the believers in the countryside with those who participated in the Boxer Rebellion but assume these believers can be better controlled.

The center of the first explosion was Henan Province. Unofficial findings indicate it could be the home of as many as 7 million Christians. It is also in Henan that the Church still thrives under severe restriction and persecution. Rarely does a month go by without the outside media confirming reports of arrests and imprisonment of Christians in Henan. Some believers have been arrested or violently beaten. Many have had to pay high fines. However, this is also where the Church is still growing the fastest.

The believers in Henan are mostly young people who have had a few years of schooling. They have returned home to join their families' struggle against poverty, backwardness, sudden de-communization and incessant natural disasters. It is a life of hardship and despair. But in the midst of that, their enthusiasm for Jesus is unparalleled. Often after work, they will gather together for hours of singing, praying and learning about God's Word. It is still common for several believers to share one Bible in Henan. Sunday gathering is a whole day, whole-family affair—several hundred people sharing their faith and food. Their immediate leaders are often new Christians. It is not uncommon for Christians less than two years old in the faith to be leading groups of more than a hundred believers. A simple belief is taught and fanned by older, more mature itinerant pastors and Christian workers who come visiting once every two or three months. These itinerant workers will stay for a few days and teach the young leaders from early morning to late at night.

The House Church has three levels of leadership. The top level is made up of the *Lao Da* (First Brothers) who are older (in their late 40s) and well-versed in the Word. They are survivors—most have prison experiences and some are still fugitives. They command much well-earned respect from the people. They develop workers, fan revival and resolve church-related issues. The *Lao Da* preach with spiritual insight and spend much time in prayer. However, they lack systematic leadership skills and exposure to the outside world and creativity to meet all the new challenges of current China, and are very cautious in developing cooperation with outsiders.

The second level is the *Lao Er* (Second Brothers). They are in their late 20s to 30s and they are also well-versed in the Word. They are often in charge of one main congregation and a number of meeting points (that is, house churches). Some are registered; some are not. Most of those at the *Lao Er* level of leadership have some prison experience. They aggressively send out teams to evangelize and plant new churches. Though they have no official connection with the Three Self Church, they are more eager to work with outsiders than those at the *Lao Da* level.

The third level is the *Lao San* (Third Brothers). They are in their 20s, and they are eager to learn everything. They are particularly hungry for systematic teaching of the Word. Their ministries, like their lifestyles, are simple and effective, done at the grass-roots level.

They are usually "tentmakers," but they are always ready to drop their "needles" and let their feet take them on a special assignment. Since they are young, they experience regular harassment from the authorities, but they usually don't get caught—"because we pray," and have a wise "Supreme Leader."

The center of the second explosion is undoubtedly Wenzhou on the coast of Taiwan Strait. The Church there has been going strong since before and during the Cultural Revolution. Their *Lao Da* would testify that while the nation bowed to Mao, Wenzhou still worshiped Jesus. The county of Wenzhou now reports that it is twenty percent Christian, with more that 2,400 churches registered as independent. Some of these churches have seating capacities of several thousand; Sunday School facilities also house thousands. Wenzhou's *Lao Da* are outstandingly aggressive. They meet openly and their young people are taught this "foreign religion."

Besides sending regular gospel bands to nearby villages, they are the ones that send out missionaries to the ethnic minorities along the borders of Russia and Burma. They also have international teams ministering in foreign countries, including Vietnam and Thailand. At home, the churches run evangelistic meetings on a weekly basis, usually Wednesday and Sunday nights. At festivals, they pack their churches with some special presentation, attracting even high-ranking officials and their families.

The leaders, particularly the *Lao Da,* have all served prison terms—some frequently, and as recently as this year. The charges are almost all violations of the "Three Designates." (The Three Self official church has a policy that only designated ministers can preach in designated churches in designated provinces.)

Until recently, the independent churches of Wenzhou did not have full-time pastors or Christian workers. The lay people, following the example of the *Lao Da,* preached everywhere in season and out of season. Thus the *Lao Da* are never deterred by government punishment, because after arrests, the churches always grow bigger.

These churches have a policy that anyone arrested for "preaching Jesus" in any form will not be bailed out. They accept the prison as their church, and they preach there. The government officials now have a policy: "Don't send Christians to jail; they are nothing but trouble. All they do is preach their gospel and too many prisoners believe. If this keeps up, we won't have any crime and our jails will be empty."

Wenzhou churches are starting to produce their own gospel tracts, songbooks, teaching materials and gospel cassettes in good-sized quantities and of professional quality. Distribution networks are far-reaching and effective. These believers are carefully meeting the needs of brothers and sisters in rural China: "We send teams to carry the materials to them and we also sponsor them to come here to pick up these gifts."

The *Lao Da's* appeal to those outside China is: "Please help develop and inform us, and stay in cooperation with us so we can better prepare our *Lao Er* and *Lao San* for both the present and the future."

The Church is aware that most of those with theological training are very old. They are equally aware that, without proper Bible training, heresy becomes a major problem. The Three Self seminaries cannot meet even the needs of their own constituents—the official Three Self Church—let alone the needs of the House Church leaders.

Because of the magnitude of the growth, the formal official institutes cannot train enough workers for China's vast and white harvest field. Other doctrines, such as teachings from outside, are swallowed without discernment by this starving body of believers. This is a critical situation! With the so-called open policy and economic reform in China, the Church is under more dangerous attacks and faces more deceptive temptations than ever before. She is reaching out to her friends and asking for help.

RENEWAL

Section Two

6

CHURCH ON
THE MARCH

"The Lord your God will drive out your enemies little by little."
—Moses

As past merges with present, Moses' admonition to God's people is appropriate to the situation in China: remember what God has done, and remember that He promises to prevail in the end. Moses also told the nation of Israel that the victory would not happen quickly, but "little by little."

God's ways are not man's ways. All of His history is one of crisis and process; the process is sometimes maddeningly slow. It involves daily drudgery and sometimes brutal persecution. This perplexes the brilliant minds of nation builders and creates tremendous discomfort for those who live in the world of "orderly process" and "instant success" like our own. We want life in this world to be assuring, like the oscilloscope beside the bed of someone critically ill that regularly "beeps" to indicate continued life; we do not want things to show us a flat line indicating that the brain is dead.

The waiting for "God to be God" is sometimes more painful and exasperating than the anguish of daily life—especially when we don't seem to feel His presence. For millions of people, today's China is not a pleasant place to live. The process of becoming a free society is perplexing and painfully slow. Those rights that so much of the world take for granted are almost non-existent in China—for the citizen in general and for believers in particular. The believers are, however, reluctant to complain.

Those who have struggled rarely speak of the struggles; they reply to inquiries about the details by simply stating, "Our Lord Jesus struggled, so why shouldn't we?"

"Struggle" was one of Mao's favorite words. The Chinese people understand that merely being a Christian can be easy and comfortable, but being a true "believer" is something altogether different.

Jesus Christ had His struggles with the Herods as well as the Caiaphases. The House Church struggles in the same way. The "Caiaphas" of China is the Religious Affairs Bureau, the official government agency committed to controlling all religious affairs. Its head, Ye Xiaowen, has no formal religious training. In China, that is not necessarily a negative factor in itself. His reputation as an atheist, however, may cause a few chopsticks to halt in mid-air.

In one of his more widely distributed letters (published by Nanjing University in 1994), he claimed that the U.S. and other Western democratic countries were "resorting to ethnic and religious issues in their attacks on China" because they are "jealous over China's economic success." Because of that jealousy, he added, "Western nations bring out their 'magic weapons' to stir up ethnic and religious conflict."

He repeatedly warned a colleague: "We still have to continue our struggle against religion." That struggle will be officially carried out through an organization for which he is responsible: the Three Self Patriotic Movement.

A more recent document, printed in an official government publication, gives little hope that things will get better any time soon. The government of Beijing will be as proficient at carrying that out as they will be in initiating the policies of the Religious Affairs Bureau. In their own words, according to their official reports, the government must control the following:

1. The daily increases in subversive activities by overseas hostile forces taking advantage of our open door policy.

2. The relaxation in recent years in the work of ideological and political indoctrination of religious believers (that is, conversions).

3. The relaxation of control of the patriotic bodies and of temples and (unregistered house) churches.

Another article calls for an "unrelenting effort in the political struggle against those forces masquerading under the cover of religion." House churches and itinerant evangelists come in for special attention: "So far as the activities of self-appointed evangelists which have sprung up among Christians in recent years, the Religious Affairs organ in every city district and outlying county must undertake political re-education and must exert themselves to uphold the Communist Party's 'Four Basic Principles,' i.e. Marxism-Leninism, Mao Zedong Thought, and sole leadership for the Party."

More specifically, a decree has been issued by the United Front Department which makes the following orders official:

1. Believers are forbidden to engage in itinerant evangelism or to preach the gospel.

2. Believers are forbidden to hold house church meetings in the villages and farms.

3. God must not be mentioned outside the doors of the TSPM churches.

4. Young people and middle-aged people are forbidden to believe in God. Only old women are allowed to believe. No one under 18 can believe, especially students.

This is official government policy and there are many Party bureaucrats in China determined to fulfill their orders. The news stories are often bad news for the Christians as they read reports like the following:

"China's religious authorities yesterday issued orders to all places of worship to register with the government. The order appeared to intensify an ongoing crackdown on religion. Church sources said several priests were detained in Beijing, Shanghai, Hebei, Anhui, Jiangxi, Zhejiang and Fujian after they refused to register last year. A number of church buildings were also torn down in Hebei, Anhui, Jiangxi and Guixhou provinces after the authorities claimed they were illegal. The warnings came as officials claimed that religion was used to subvert the state. The Chinese News agency Xinhua said there were three immediate tasks required to clean up problems with religion:

1. To order all places of worship to register.
2. To deal with difficult religious problems of public concern.
3. To cultivate contingents of young patriotic religious preachers."[1]

Add to this the firm belief by some Party officials that the fall of Marxism-Leninism in Eastern Europe is directly attributable to a Christian spiritual revival. A high-ranking official said that China oppressed the Christian Church because, "We have seen what they, together with foreign, unfriendly forces, have done to Poland, Hungary, and the Soviet Union. We do not want that to happen in our country." There is a bit of irony in that the world's leading atheist power gives proper credit where it belongs for what happened in Europe, and defines the struggle as spiritual rather than political.

Confirmation of how committed Mr. Ye and his staff at the Religious Affairs Bureau are, not just in dotting every 'i' but in crossing every 't', is given each day as these news reports from China indicate:

"Sources say tensions between security forces and house churches throughout the central provinces of Henan and Anhui have escalated in recent months, with an increase in police surveillance of house church activities, confiscation of Bibles and arbitrary fines imposed on house church members.

"In late September, sources said security officials in the northwestern Anhui county of Lixin arrested and imprisoned two house church Christians after 'falsely accusing' them of leaking information about police/house church tensions to 'anti-China overseas organizations.'

"The two church members were given two-year 're-education through labor' prison sentences and have been sent to a coal mining labor reform camp in Xuancheng, southeastern Anhui.

"Sources say Public Security Bureau (PSB) senior officials in Lixin were angered over the international media attention that followed the arrests and imprisonment of six house church leaders from Lixin and the adjoining county of Mengcheng in late 1993.

"Several of the church leaders were given two-year prison sentences for offenses as minor as possessing a Bible that had been printed abroad and organizing groups of Christians to listen to Hong Kong Christian radio broadcasts.

"Under the Chinese government's 'Three Designates' religious policy, only designated registered church personnel may preach at a designated registered religious venue in a designated province.

"Six house church leaders from the central Chinese province of Henan were sentenced without trial on August 14, 1994 to three years imprisonment after being accused of membership in an outlawed religious sect and participation in anti-government activities.

"According to Hong Kong's *South China Morning Post*, the six Christian leaders were taken into custody during a police crackdown on unregistered house churches in Henan's Zhoukou region in June. A total of sixty-eight Christians were arrested during the crackdown."

There are also new efforts to register all Christian meetings in China, as the following indicates:

"A January 31, 1994 State Council religious dictum ordered that all sites of religious activity register with the Bureau. Several months later, China's Religious Affairs Bureau issued national regulations outlining the procedures that unsanctioned religious groups must follow to have their meeting places registered by the government.

"While the procedures were aimed at standardizing the process of religious registration, they contained a number of elements that analysts said were problematic for the country's unregistered house church Christians. For example, according to Hong Kong's Chinese Church Research Center, church groups are required to accept the government's narrowly defined interpretation of 'legitimate' religious activity before they can qualify for registration.

"Many house church leaders have argued that to register with the government would compromise their religious faith by giving ultimate authority to the state. They also fear it would open their members to numerous restrictions.

"According to China's Xinhua news agency, the new registration order came as government officials claimed that religion was being used to subvert the state. 'Those who make use of religion to interfere with administrative, judicial, martial, educational and other social affairs, especially those who take advantage of religious reasons to split the country, must be severely cracked down upon according to law,' Xinhua news agency quoted State Councilor Ismail Amat as saying."

Sometimes the results are more a throwback to the days of the Cultural Revolution:

"According to a first-hand account by one of the victims, Xu Fang, a 21 year old woman from Ankang County, the police attacked a group of worshippers at a religious meeting on March 27, 1993. This account was made available to Asia Watch by Protestant church sources. Eight or nine Public Security Bureau officers broke into the gathering and 'without a word of explanation began to beat us with rods and put handcuffs on the five who came from Ankang,' three men and two women. These five were singled out because authorities suspected them of connections with foreigners.

"They stripped three brethren naked from the waist and forced the women to stand with them. Not only did these authorities beat them, moreover they forced each of the twenty-six other local people to beat each one 100 times with bamboo rods. If they refused, the authorities would in turn beat them. The three were beaten until they were totally covered with blood, gaping wounds and injuries all over their bodies. As if such violent beating wasn't enough, they then hanged them up and with the rods began to hit them on their backs. They did this until they were unconscious and barely breathing. We could only hear the sound of the beating and the cursing of the officers.

"The two women from Ankang were also violently beaten. They passed out, and when they awoke they found that: 'Two of us sisters had been placed on the stove and a large millstone of over 100 catties (130 pounds) was placed on our backs while they continued to beat us with rods. They also . . . ripped open our pants . . . using the most cruel methods to beat our private parts.'

"The following morning, the victims were sent to the Taoyuan police station and then taken to the Public Security Bureau in Liuia. But the officers there refused to accept them and sent them back to Taoyuan where they remained for eight days under the most primitive conditions. After the officers realized the extent of Lai's injuries, a doctor was called to provide minimal medical treatment.

"The guards realized he was about to die and made him leave the room. He struggled, walking some and crawling some for ten kilometers . . . he just collapsed. The local people found him and carried him to a small house, but after one day and night he died.

"After members of his family, hearing he had been released, found his body by the roadside, they began to make inquiries at the Xunyang PSB. According to a police autopsy, Lai died of an illness."

While persecution of the house church continues, we can be certain of two things: the itinerant evangelist will continue to be itinerant, and the house church will continue to grow.

It should be pointed out that the churches sanctioned by the official TSPM and found in most major cities have been and continue to be evangelical. Their members, and often their pastors, have made a very positive contribution to the revival in China. This contribution may become less defined as new pastors are trained at the official theological seminaries in China, which are under the control of the TSPM, and replace the older pastors who filled the pulpits starting in the early 1980s out of necessity rather than choice.

The official Three Self Church parallels in many ways the National Association of Evangelicals (NAE) and similar evangelical organizations in the U.S. While it is a governing body, the TSPM leadership in Beijing would be more akin in theology and practice to our National Council of Churches and similar ecumenical organizations. Rather than preaching the absolute truth of Jesus Christ, it is more concerned with its position of authority.

How does the Church respond to these attempts to intimidate?

"We are like a great prairie fire. When they step on us, sparks fly and the tinder, the dry hearts of socialists are lighted, and a new flame starts. You cannot stop a revival unless the believers rebel against God, and that, God forbid, we shall not do. The government is helpless. After all, what can they do to us that they have not already done? It is like our Lord Jesus Christ said: 'I will build my Church and the gates of hell shall not prevail against it.'"

Recently, a government official stood over a small figure sitting in a chair. He hit the desk with his fist and spit out the words, "You have got to stop meeting. There are now 98 million of you."[2] He caught himself, but too late. He had mistakenly, in a moment of anger, given to a house church leader the government figure for the number of believers in China. The number was significant— and it is double the size of the membership of the Communist party.

The Communist official, like the house church leader, knows that the growth cannot be stopped any more than a person can put out a prairie fire with a wet gunnysack. Jesus' words, "I will build my Church and the gates of hell will not prevail against it," are coming to life each day in China—not by the hundreds but by the thousands, not just in the villages but in the cities as well.

It is a Church with an agenda, and it now has two goals:

1. Turn China into a Christian nation like, as they say, "America used to be."

2. Make China the largest sending nation of missionaries in the world by the year 2005.

The army of God is well on its way to fulfilling its vision. The invitation has gone out to thousands of Chinese Christians overseas—professionals, doctors, scientists, computer experts—to return to the motherland and use their expertise in evangelizing the world. And many are heeding the call.

As for sending missionaries, there are hundreds already in the countries surrounding China, and Muslims dominate many of those countries. There is the question of obtaining visas.

"Visas? What are they?" one Christian missionary responded. Then looking down at the ground, he took a step forward and exclaimed, "Brother, we have two feet. That is all we need—our feet, and this." He held up his Bible. "Jesus didn't tell us we needed a visa. He just said 'go.' We obey His command and go, two by two. We do not carry a purse, extra clothing or shoes. We greet no one along the way. God leads us to a home and as we enter we know whether or not we are welcome."

Procuring a visa or making preparations for being welcomed are as foreign to these missionaries as doing deputation to raise support for housing and cost of living expenses.

Several areas of China's church growth need further consideration. Some are negative and some are very positive. Let's look at them one by one.

Notes:

1. *News Network International—News Service,* January 1996.
2. Figures vary as to the numerical size of the Church. House church leaders are not as concerned with the numbers as with the quality of the individual believers.

7

CHRISTIAN
HERESY

"You were running well; who hindered you from obeying the truth?"
—Paul

The Church's explosive growth without second generation leadership is not without problems. At the top of the list of problems is heresy.

A man who had fallen away from the Lord fell into an old well while walking through a field, and landed on his head. The well was not big enough to turn around in, so he started praying: "Lord, if you will get me out of here, I will follow you forever." He called out for help, but he knew it was useless. No one ever came by that deserted place. The blood continued to rush to his head, and he was getting too weak to cry for help. Suddenly, he heard voices, and it wasn't long before he felt a rope around his legs. Soon he was pulled out, laid down on the ground, and breathing fresh air. Now he heads a group of more than 10,000 people who believe that the only way to pray is while standing on your head. What the Communists cannot do to the church, this kind of heresy can. Trouble comes not only from the atheists who say there is no God; it also arrives through those who have adopted some strange—and in many cases anti-Christian—concepts because of a lack of Bible training.

Ron MacMillan, theologian and Asian journalist with News

Network International, reports:

"Another heresy with serious consequences was discovered in
the central province of Hubei in 1988. Two travelers from a Hong
Kong evangelical mission ran into a distraught young man with
blood running from his nose as he kept pounding his palm into
his forehead. He was muttering, 'I must hear the voice, I must
hear the voice . . .' After calming down he told them that his
church elders had given him until the 22nd of the month to hear
the voice of God. If he did not hear the voice he would be eter-
nally damned. No wonder he was distraught. It was 9:30 p.m. on
the night of the 21st. The visitors later learned that he had committed suicide. This young man belonged to what is sometimes
known as the 'audible voice cult.' In the early 1980s, its founder
had been given one page of Scripture. The fragment was a page
from the book of Acts, specifically chapter nine, the story of the
apostle Paul's conversion experience on the road to Damascus.
The pastor concluded, 'This is how we know we are saved, when
Jesus speaks audibly to us.'"[1]

As the pastor's movement has developed, newly appointed
elders have reportedly abused their powers by saying to certain
troubled souls, "You must hear the voice by this date, otherwise
you cannot join us, and you cannot be saved." The cult, now
numbering in the thousands in many provinces, has a suspi-
ciously high suicide rate among its adherents.

A third example of heresy comes from the revival province
itself—Henan, where there are an estimated 10 million
Christians. A certain movement, which goes by various names,
requires individuals to participate in a three-day induction period
that takes place in a darkened room, because leaders teach that the
Holy Spirit falls on His people more easily when all the lights are
out. The three days are intensive. First they learn about the
church. They are told that the "true" interpretation of the parable
of the talents, found in Matthew 25, is that "those who are full-

time workers have five talents; those who are semi-full-time have two talents, and ordinary people have just one." Instructors emphasize the importance of five talents— "for then your reward will be greatest."

Yet despite its elitism and exclusivity, the movement is reportedly aggressively evangelistic. Some tens of thousands in Henan now claim to be members, and there are thought to be more than 2,000 evangelists in other provinces spreading their message. An itinerant evangelist from northern Jiangsu, however, complained, "It's a tragedy that they go only to other churches to steal sheep; they never go to non-Christians and try to make converts to Christ!"

These heretical sects represent a progression. The first heresy came about as a result of an unusual experience which, in the absence of mature leadership and Bibles, took hold and spread. The second was actually based on Scripture, but without the whole Bible an unbalanced message resulted. The third sect had the Scriptures, yet spread their heresy from ignorance and pride.

One fact is clear: heresy has taken such root in China's Church that it is no longer caused merely by the number of conversions outstripping the Church's resources to disciple.

On a June trip to China, extending from Kunming in the deep south to Beijing in the north, we interviewed twelve key house church leaders, eleven of whom confirmed that heresy, in their opinion, is "the major problem facing the Church in China today." Eight used the word "crisis."

One of the Beijing leaders said, "Whenever you get revival you expect a Satanic response, and the fostering of heresy is a predictable tactic, so we are not surprised to see the incidence of heresy. But what really concerns us is that current conditions in China for heresy to flourish are so ideal that the gains of the entire revival could be reversed."

Discernible in their explanation of the spread of revival were two sets of factors which can be labeled "inevitable" and "avoidable." The first refer to those conditions that are endemic to any revival anywhere, where the explosive growth makes the adequate discipling of new converts a major headache—especially in a closed society—thus leaving the door open for heresy.

The second set of factors, the avoidable ones, is more significant. They represent either weaknesses that are not being addressed or deliberate policies, either in the Church or in the state, that actually give heresy impetus. A Shanghai house church leader said, "It's partly our fault that heresy is spreading at the rate it is."

It would be wrong to say that people can come to Christ too quickly for the good of the Body of Christ, but some Chinese Christians are tempted to think that way today. If the Chinese revival is growing at the rate of possibly 20,000 people per day, a discipling challenge is posed on a scale unique to Christendom.

Then there are the problems that being an enormous and backward country imposes. People are too poor to travel to discipleship classes. Most people in the countryside have barely finished grammar school, and illiteracy runs as high as eighty percent in some rural provinces. So circulating books is of limited value.

Considering that these new converts also come from a shamanistic background, where witchcraft and acts of sorcery are common, it is very hard, in the absence of good teaching, for them to quickly leave their superstitious habits behind.

Heresy also serves as an excuse for the government to suppress all "religion and superstition." It does not make a fine distinction between the two. A recent report from Human Rights Watch/Asia, entitled *China: Persecution of a Protestant Sect*, documents the repression of a sect called the "Shouters." This sect was allegedly started and headed by a Chinese who lived in the U.S.

but has now passed away—Li Chang Shou, better known as Witness Lee. Though he was once a disciple of Watchman Nee, the similarities end there. The point is not to argue the validity of the "Shouters" and their theology, but rather to notice that the government considers it to be "a foreign connection." The suppression could be a blueprint for the suppression of any other Christian group.

Before one becomes too critical of the Chinese government, one must remember that it does believe that Christianity was responsible for the overthrow of Marxism in Europe. More importantly than that, the government is quick to remind the people of how Christian heresy turned the country upside down a century ago.

Ron MacMillan summarizes it this way:

"In 1836, a young man named Hong Xiuquan received a tract from a Protestant missionary. He kept the tract for six years without looking at it, but then one morning he had a strange dream in which he met a bearded man whom he called 'elder brother.' This man gave him a sword and instructed him in the art of slaying evil spirits. Upon waking, he picked up the tract and made the connection. The man in the dream was Jesus Christ, and Hong must be his younger brother.

"By 1849 he had 10,000 followers; by 1850, 20,000. By 1853 he was on the warpath. His heavenly calling inspired his followers to fight, and that year they captured the great city of Nanking and controlled a large section of southern China. The Peking government panicked and enlisted foreign armies to put down the Taiping Rebellion, as it came to be known, in 1864.

"The Chinese have long memories, and the origins of the Taiping Rebellion are well known to its current leaders. With the events of Eastern Europe bringing home the power of the Church in promoting political change, China's leaders are understandably nervous about the potential of heretical movements; they are likewise paranoid about those with an anti-government emphasis."

However, it must be recognized that most house church leaders reckon that heresy is, at the moment, a potential rather than an actual danger; they are confident that the Church will not be devastated by it. The major Hong Kong-based evangelical ministries are basically in agreement with this, and all run large-scale projects to give a thorough theological education to house church pastors and evangelists. The dangers are obvious, but confidence is high. This confidence comes from the unique post-war Chinese Christian experience.

As one house church evangelist in Shanghai put it, "We faced Mao's Cultural Revolution in the 60s, and triumphed; now we are facing the devil's sorcery revolution—this will be harder to win!" But, he added, "The Chinese Church is not through with the fire; we have learned a spiritual lesson from the Cultural Revolution that will carry us through this revolution, and that is that God tests His people with fire!"

Notes:

1.   Special report by Ron MacMillan, *News Network International,* 1990.

8

SLAUGHTER OF INNOCENTS

"Be fruitful and multiply . . ."
—God

" In our day," the old man observed sagely, "we did not walk so close together, and we certainly did not hold hands in public."

His wife deliberately reached over and took his callused hand, smiled and said with a voice full of many different emotions, "Things . . . have changed."

At that moment, one of those "changes" caused an abrupt separation between a young man and his love who were walking together close by. They distanced themselves from each other as she cried out emphatically, "But I want a family, a boy and a girl!"

He reached for her hand again and held it in his as they resumed their walk. This time, she hung her head sadly as he mutely looked ahead.

The couple found little comfort in knowing that their problem was not unique. It was the same burden shared by 150 million other young people who wanted to marry and have a family. There was no excited chatter about wedding invitations and bridal gowns, no discussions about receptions and where they would honeymoon. They had a much more difficult issue to discuss.

They had just finished another of the pre-marital educational sessions that the government required before it would grant a marriage license. They had also already undergone the compulsory pre-marital medical exam to determine if either suffered from a "genetic disorder" or serious disease. Government doctors gave them the results—neither had a serious disease and no member of either family had a mental disorder; therefore, no sterilization would be required before the marriage. All seemed to be in order, but they still faced the next major hurdle.

"I almost wish I did have a crazy uncle so I would be sterilized—then the decision would be made for us," the young woman told her beloved.

"No, don't say that," he implored. "We want children. We need a son, but we also want a daughter. Any child born to us will be a special gift." He faced her again and took her hands in his. "Look! what we want is impossible. We can only have one child unless we move to the countryside. You are a teacher. I am an engineer. We could both lose our jobs if we have more than one child."

"And of course that child has to be a boy!"

They slowly drew apart again. He stuck his hands deep into his pockets as they continued their walk. They knew the law. The Premier himself had announced on television that those who violate the one child policy must be punished— "severely punished." He told the people that, with a population of 1.2 billion, they must be more forceful in the campaign to limit children.

Another official had then appeared on camera. She explained in a kind, grandmotherly fashion that it wasn't really a problem. "We will help you keep under the limit. There are more than 1 million family planning associations in our country and 330,000 regular workers available to help you implement the new program. There will be no charge. It is part of the government's concern for your well-being." As the official switched into the Premier's mode of speaking, the TV camera captured well the sudden disappearance of the warm smile: "The plan will be forcefully implemented." The smile returned as she reminded them, "In addition to the government specialists, 80 million birth control volunteers are ready to be of assistance—especially for newlyweds and young couples anticipating marriage."

The young woman's voice had been severe as she talked back to the television screen: "Well, what if the first child is a girl? That wonderful government of ours has imported 75,000 new sonogram machines to help us know if we've produced a boy or a girl. They'll share that piece of important information with us AND with the local family planning leader. What if it is a girl?" Both man and woman knew the one statistic the counselor did not enunciate: 97.5 % of abortions in China are performed on female fetuses.

They also had heard terrible reports that they knew to be true. For example, a village woman was practically lauded in the newspaper, and certainly not condemned, for drowning five of her newborn children because they were girls. She wanted to be a "good citizen" and give her husband a son.

The young couple knew what advice they would receive from the counselors. In the cities, abortions were not only available on demand; they were demanded. It didn't matter at what point the pregnancy was ended. In fact, doctors understood the "problem" and would see to it that a babe was born "dead."

In the villages, the father or the neighbors would take care of the details if no doctor was available.

"Well, if we have a girl, she won't have any problem finding a husband. The counselors forgot to mention that there are twenty-nine single men for every single woman between the ages of 25 and 49," the young man said.

"Yeah, like in Yunnan—a hundred eligible bachelors, but not one single girl to marry. We are going to be a society of men only."

They stopped to sit on a grassy slope. He leaned back and put his hands behind his neck; she sat looking up into the sky.

"What a wonderful society we have here," he said sarcastically. "We fall in love. We want to get married. They test us to see that there are no crazies in our background, no syphilis, no AIDS. So aren't we fortunate! Neither of us has to be sterilized. So we get married, have our first child, and if it's discovered that we will have a girl we can have a free abortion."

"Or, we can have our little girl . . . and . . ."

"Well, we could move to the farm. We both have uncles and aunties who live on farms . . . we could have a second child then. Maybe it will be a boy."

"And if it's not?"

"Try again?"

"Sure, like our good cousin, and pay the government 2,000 yuan—twenty months' salary! No, thank you."

She leaned over and gently stroked his face. "Boy or girl, I want your child, and I want to be your wife." He didn't move. "Well, at least help with suicide is free, too." They looked at each other and neither was smiling.

The frustrating cycle continues for millions of young people. The campaign started with weeding out the retarded. With pride, the government announced that during the past four years, in Gansu province alone, 260,000 people labeled "retarded" were sterilized.

The healthy get married, but they can have only one child if they live in a city. They can have only two children if they live in the countryside. A free abortion is available for any more pregnancies, available up until the hour of birth. If the child is allowed to live, the parents could be labeled "reactionaries."

The older couple on the park bench thought back over the problems their generation had faced—and the problems they had yet to face as the older generation. They had had their own moments of apprehension. Recently, there was a statement in the newspaper by a government official about the "old people of our country." That statement made the park bench feel more like a seat of doom than a place of rest. One didn't need a post-marital counseling session to understand that the official government statements meant planned execution—from sterilization, to abortion, to infanticide, to euthanasia.

The tragic irony is that the policies are being perpetrated and supported by the very same people who seethe at the very mention of Adolph Hitler's name. Yet they are fulfilling a major part of his *Mein Kampf*—and there is no one to abort their plans.

Where does God fit into this picture?

Genesis tells us that earth and seed go together like love and marriage. When God cradled a measure of earth in His sacred hands and breathed on it, the breath of God entered man. Since then, every seed is sacred and part of His handiwork, and His breath will be there from fertilization to death, when the dust will return to the earth and the breath will realize its eternal destiny.

Chinese believers courageously struggle to live out their convictions. They refuse to have abortions and choose to pay the consequences instead. God has not forgotten them, as the following graphically illustrates.

A new itinerant evangelist was traveling on foot from village to village in China at Christmas. He had already made quite a few converts in the first five villages, and he was approaching the sixth.

Little did he know that he was about to experience a drama that, in retrospect, seemed like a replay of Bethlehem itself. This is the story in his own words:

"Greetings!" I called to a group of villagers. "I am a bearer of good news. The —"

A man interrupted me: "We have only bad news here," he said irritably. "A couple has just had their baby stolen."

In China, where couples are restricted by law to having only one child, the kidnapping and selling of babies is not uncommon. I asked to see the couple, thinking I might help. I found them despondent.

"'I'm so sorry," I said. "But I know someone who can help you—God. Let me pray to Him on your behalf."

There was no reaction on their sad faces. I went into prayer anyway, feeling very uncomfortable: "Dear Father, many years ago at this same time of year You sent a child into the world and rescued us all. I ask that You bring back this couple's child and deliver this village from sadness. Amen."

Suddenly the young father spoke, "Shut up and go away. We have prayed to our gods and nothing has happened. Why should yours be any different?" People then grabbed me roughly and forced me to leave the village.

I felt like such a failure as I wandered in a daze of humiliation and tears, crying out to God. Then I thought about Christmas. The Son of God had come into the world knowing He would be despised, beaten, misunderstood, and then crucified. Yet He came. I thought how I had come into the village expecting a hero's welcome. Instead, I had been treated a little like Christ was treated.

I knew then that I had to return to the village, though I'd be despised, but following in my Master's footsteps, bringing His

Good News. He had the courage. So must I.

Frightened, I walked back slowly. Suddenly across the still, late afternoon air, I heard a baby's cry coming from the shaft of an old well. Looking down, I saw that the baby's face was blue. I climbed in to hug some warmth into it and realized then that it had been left to die because it was a girl. People who buy kidnapped babies in China only want boys.

As I approached the village, people came running, overjoyed at the sight of the baby. When I saw the mother, the smile on her face seemed almost holy. "Come, warm yourself by the fire," said the father. "Who was that God you prayed to?" they now asked.

The couple believed in Jesus that night, and I learned a great lesson too. I had only heard the baby's cry because I had turned to go back to the village. If I hadn't had the courage to take the gospel in spite of the danger, I would have walked in a different direction and missed finding the baby.

I gained great insight that Christmas into the courage of Jesus. He came willingly, knowing the hatred and harm ahead. My prayer now is, "God, grant me more of the courage that made Christmas possible."

The above story illustrates the direction the church in China will continue to walk. Whether the message of His love is given in the parks, the city streets via an itinerant evangelist, or by radio, God's people in China are spreading the Good News that God came to earth as a child to bring hope and salvation to all people—Christmas is every day.

9

WOMEN OF INTEGRITY

"Women hold up half of the sky."
—Mao Zedong

Women came from all over the world. They were dressed in native attire and speaking many tongues, but they came with one stated purpose: to write another chapter of the age-old battle of the sexes. The United Nations Conference on Women was held in Beijing. For days they argued with each other, tested the patience of Chinese hospitality and made statements for the world press.

There was talk about sexual freedom, sexual slavery, sexual harassment and sexual exploitation. However, one subject was hardly mentioned: men. Enormous lengths were taken to avoid acknowledging their existence. The notable exception was a vitriolic criticism of what they called the "Nazi stormtroopers"—the sometimes bemused, often confused, Chinese security police. They were meticulously careful in their language. They referred to "chairpersons," and they called for the elimination of "gender-based violence" rather than male brutality. Interpreters worked long into the night to find new words to describe the unmentionable. It was a contentious struggle between the politically and the ideologically correct.

If one was to believe the final communiqué, it was all about "equality, development and peace," with statements like, "If the world were run by the will of women, there would be no wars because women are peace-loving people."

In the end, they left town with a piece of paper which did little to settle that age-old battle. The Beijing meeting was, after all, just a routine conference; next year there would be another one in another exotic location, and there would be another declaration similar to those made in Cairo, Nairobi, and Mexico City.

The irony, though, was that if they had strayed beyond the klieg lights of the world press and the rasping voice of Bella Abzug, they would have seen a nation where women have indeed made tremendous advances—all 600 million of them.

Instead of reviling China, if the delegates had taken a closer look at their host country, they would have seen that it has made tremendous changes in the role of women. Even more importantly, they would have noted that the greatest progress for women's rights was made in the one institution that most of the Beijing delegates held in contempt: Christianity in general and evangelical Christianity in particular.

Had they talked to any believers in China, instead of echoing each other's whining and often venomous rhetoric, they would have seen that the greatest liberator of women in all history was, and still is, Jesus Christ—a man, but more than that: He is the Light in the darkness. Two thousand years ago, and again in this generation, darkness refused the intrusion of light into its personal agenda.

Had they looked, they would have seen that an old Chinese religion, Confucianism, taught that women were in every way inferior to men and totally subordinate to their husbands. A Confucian proverb says that if a son was born he should be given a piece of jade to play with. But if by some terrible act of nature the child was a girl, she should be given a broken piece of pottery. The women at the UN Conference repeated history. They turned from both the jade and the pottery to try and remold their own piece of broken clay.

Had the delegates inquired, they would have learned that in China, there is one place where a boy or girl is considered a gift from God. Though the ultrasound reveals a child will be a girl, she is not aborted. Further, the delegates would have seen that for house church believers, raising all the children God gives them is the norm—though this is not true for China in general.

Had the delegates gotten beyond discussions of inequalities, they might have seen that when the missionaries (whom they call "culture destroyers") brought the Gospel of Jesus Christ to China, they also brought the message that men and women are equal in God's sight. The missionaries knew and believed that medical care and education were needed by both.

As in previous meetings, the body of believers was totally ignored in Beijing, as were other relevant facts. For example, it was Christian missionaries who opened the first school for women in Ningbo, China, in 1844. Sixty years later, China's Christians had established missionary colleges for women in Beijing, Fuzhou, and Nanjing, a move that would later be countenanced as "very wise" by the government, which then built similar schools. The Christian missionaries also fought against the traditional practice of binding women's feet—a cruel practice that symbolized female bondage in a male-dominated society. Even antagonistic delegates would have given credit to the missionaries for breaking down this cultural inequality—if they had looked beyond the dictated agenda. But even though they had "eyes to see and ears to hear," they did neither.

Fortunately for them, the Christian Gospel went far beyond the comfortable venues of women's conferences. It reached into cities and the countryside with teaching at the grass-roots level of the sacredness of marriage. This in turn helped to stamp out the evils of child brides and prostitution.

Any historian or conference delegate who was not blinded by his or her own prejudices could have seen, with only cursory inquiry, that women have always possessed a prominent role in the Church in China. Even before Mao, at least sixty percent of all missionaries in China were women. The history of the Church literally glows with the presence of China's "Bible Women." These women were in many cases the forerunners of later mission stations. As early as 1878, the Reformed Church in Amoy sent out these extraordinary "liberated women" two by two to evangelize the surrounding villages. They went without purse, without special food, without the press, and without any agenda except spreading their Lord's gospel.

These Bible Women and their counterparts—the everyday wives and mothers—played an immeasurable role in preserving the Church and causing it to grow during the dark days of Mao's regime and the Cultural Revolution, which was led in no small part by Madam Mao.

Many of the male pastors were imprisoned and it was the women of the church who carried the flaming torch of the gospel. Fired by fervent and burning prayer, they were people of extraordinary ability in evangelism.

Today, those Bible Women, still a tremendous inspiration, are replaced by their younger counterparts—none of whom have ever been to a United Nations conference. They are not even aware that they were considered "oppressed victims." They are simply "evangelists."

Consider Mama Ling. Mama Ling was a first-generation Bible Woman. Her adopted daughter was second generation. Together they established more than thirty-five churches in three coastal provinces.

Mama Ling became a Christian when she worked as an *amah*, a nanny, for a Shanghai Christian family. When she became a Christian, she was determined to read the Bible for herself, so the housewife and the children taught her how to read and write.

One of the children, now a Christian leader in Hong Kong, still remembers teaching Mama Ling to read the Bible from the Gospel of Mark: "She spent hours late at night learning the characters and memorizing the Scripture." Later, his mother released Mama Ling back to her village so she could fulfill her "calling" as an evangelist. "My mother saw in her a special gifting for winning people to the Lord," he said. "Even when Mama Ling was working for us, she was winning other *amahs* in the neighborhood to Jesus."

Mama Ling did not stay in her own village for long. After she established a small church there, she and her adopted daughter went to another village to begin a new ministry. Then they traveled from village to village as itinerant Bible Women. From time to time they went back to Shanghai to spend some time with their old employer.

"Every time they came back, my mother and all of us children would surround Mama Ling and ask her to tell us stories of her work," the man recalls. The things that stand out in his memory are the "signs and wonders" that followed Mama Ling. "She told of people coming to Jesus after they were healed or had evil spirits cast out from them. Then they burned their idols and images of their gods and formed a gathering point to worship Jesus. Mama Ling could tell the gospel to the rural people with so much emotion and drama that people would cry out, loudly repenting of their sins."

Upon one of Mama Ling's later visits to Shanghai, she met up with the Christian leader from Hong Kong whom she had nursed when he was a baby. She told him that her adopted daughter had also become an evangelist. "She's married to Jesus," she told him. Her daughter had been sentenced to a labor camp in Anhui, and had died there four years before. "But before she was arrested, my daughter and I traveled everywhere preaching the gospel. We linked up with two elderly pastors, and they followed up with secret baptism for the new believers."

Mama Ling is now in her mid-80s, living alone in a village near Shanghai. "Don't call me a Bible Woman. I am not worthy of this title. I am just an *amah* for Jesus." Today, she still conducts small-group training sessions for younger Chinese Bible Women.

Any one of the thousands of UN convention delegates could have visited an official Three Self Church and seen for themselves that many of the TSPM pastors are women—nearly fourteen percent. In twelve of the officially approved theological seminaries, women outnumber those that the convention considers unmentionables—men. It is estimated that seventy percent of active Christian believers in China today are women, and in many churches ninety percent are women.

Granted, "women's liberation" is still a difficult issue in China, especially when it involves the government's infamous one child policy. The tragedy is in the tone of the UN conference. Women from all over the world—women who were honestly and rightfully seeking their proper place in society—met in the capital of a country where equality with men is a fact of life, not just a position on paper. Yet the delegates left town oblivious to the fact that the best advocate women have ever had—regardless of race, language or culture—is the One who directs the lives of so many women of China: He is The Lord Jesus Christ.

During the Cultural Revolution, as the men were sent to prison or to labor reform camps, many women were left behind. The ensuing hardships were no less than their husbands' had been; sometimes they were even worse. Their existence may not have entailed as much physical pain (though many women in prison were treated worse than men, and often by women), but they faced the daily anxiety of sustaining a home under terribly difficult circumstances.

I listened to a couple who were back together after being separated by the husband's long imprisonment. They sat on the side of a hotel bed, small and frail, but glowing with godly countenances. They looked more like brother and sister than husband and wife. Like so many others I'd interviewed, they did not dwell on persecution; instead, they focused on privilege. As the wife began her story, the words were sometimes haltingly spoken as tears welled up for both of them. They would smile at each other and tighten their grip on each other's hands and then she would quietly continue with their story:

"It all happened rather suddenly, but yet it was expected: the Communist cadre had come into our house. Inside were six children, my husband and I, and my mother-in-law. We were afraid when we heard that knock on the door. They'd come to cleanse one more 'bad element' from Mao's revolution and we knew that cleansing would involve my husband. The Red Guard grabbed him and took him away. In a matter of days, signs appeared denouncing him. His long-time friends and neighbors stood up and called him a traitor to the revolution in order to save themselves. Some of them said he received money from Christians in America. Others said he read a book from foreign countries. That was the Bible. He was told that if he would just stand up and publicly denounce his Christianity he would be free to return to his family. But of course, he refused. And like thousands before him, he was sentenced to prison for thought reform.

"Left at home, I too was labeled a parasite. I had to wear the stigma of my anti-revolutionary husband. Well, it was very difficult to survive during those days. And I think there are four pressures I would like to share with you that I went through during those many years that my husband was in prison.

"That first pressure was supplying the needs of our family of six children, my mother-in-law and myself. My income was eighty cents a day. My life was like Elijah's; I just didn't know what to do. One night I had nothing to feed my children; I had nothing to feed myself. Remember now, we were 'parasites.' My husband is what they called a bad element, an anti-revolutionary. He's in prison.

"My children could no longer play with their schoolmates. In fact, they couldn't go to school any more. Dunce caps were put on my children and they were marched down the street while the other children threw stones at them. The mental pressure on these children was probably greater than the physical pressure. But there I was, my cupboards were bare. I called out, 'Lord, I have nothing but two drinking bottles of water. What shall I do?'

"I lay there tossing and listening to my children and my mother-in-law sleeping. We only had this one room where everyone slept. I cried out, 'God, what am I to do?' I think He was saying, 'Nothing. Just let Me do something.' I still didn't go to sleep.

"At five minutes to six—I remember the time in the morning—I heard a knock on the door. This was unusual since it was so early. I thought, *'It's probably the party leader coming to tell me my husband has received his proper reward.'* This was the jargon for being executed or dying in prison.

"As I opened the door, very frightened, there stood a lady about 60 years old—a complete stranger. She said to me as she looked around, 'I have been working very hard to find you. I walked all night. I have been moved by the Spirit to give you this.' And she handed me an envelope and then quickly left. I have not seen her since. I opened the envelope and inside was 50 yuan (US$9). That was enough for two months worth of food. I cried as I realized that God would take care of us. I went back to bed and slept for a while.

"During the next years, I never worried again about food. Every month someone, somehow, would either send me money in the mail or quietly slip it under my door. I don't know how, but I'll tell you this, we never missed one meal during those twenty-one years. We never had anything left over, but we never lacked for food. How did I handle it, you ask? I didn't. I let the Lord handle it. We were His children and He provided our daily bread.

"The second pressure was work. I was at the mercy of the cadre leaders. They could do anything they wanted to me. I was a drag on society. I was what they called a bad person. Well, I was working in an office. As you can see, I'm not a very big person. I only weigh 125 pounds. One day a big sign appeared on my door and in several other places throughout the village. It said, 'Mrs. So-and-So is now working in a comfortable office. She should not be working there because she is a counterrevolutionary.' In other words, my job was too comfortable for me.

"A week later I was pushing a wheelbarrow with 750 kilograms of bricks and mud. That's 250 pounds each. My hands were raw and bleeding. I had never done this kind of work before. It was seven days a week from early morning until late at night. We would sweat in the summer and freeze in the winter. But it was always outside work. When I complained, they gave me a shovel and two cement buckets to shovel cement into these buckets, and then carry them up to the second floor of a building. To some they would say, 'You're working too hard. You're tired, rest a while.' But they never said that to me. I was a bad element.

"How did I survive? Well, my hands healed. I got muscles where I didn't have them before. But I learned about the mercy of the Lord. Somehow He helped me. Not a day at a time, but a brick at a time, and a bucket of cement at a time. They could see that I was not going to buckle under. I would not give them the satisfaction. All I would tell them was that my Lord is sufficient. That made them very, very angry.

"So then they applied political pressure. After a long day of work they would take me to a building where I had to sit alone, and men and women would surround me and shout at me. They would say, 'Cut all connections with your husband. If you do not, both of you will deserve to sit on the same bench.' That is to say, we would both suffer the same fate—prison. Another would shout, 'Give up your faith!' Another would shout in my face, 'Heaven cannot give you bread down here! Only Mao Zedong can give you bread! He is the bread for your life! Stand on the side of the people,' they would say. 'Don't be a traitor, confess your sins. Cut all connections with your husband.' And of course they also wanted to know where I got the money to buy food for my children and mother-in-law. I really didn't know, so I couldn't tell them.

"Let me say that if I had not had Jesus, I would have committed suicide. Two others killed themselves who were on the same bench. Another went insane and is still that way today. But I would just close my eyes and pray. I knew the Lord had nothing against me. He preserved me.

"They did this six hours a day—late, late into the night—for six months, seven days a week. And finally they gave up. They just left me alone. God wouldn't let them break me. And one of the Communist leaders looked at me and said, 'You say that you forgive those who struggled against you, but we want you to know that we will never forgive you.' However, he told me I was being given another chance to repent. They took me from the brick factory and the cement factory and sent me back with my scarred hands to the office to work. The Lord had won another battle.

"The fourth pressure came because I was still a fairly attractive 39 year old lady when the head of my struggle committee wanted a wife: me. He made it sound so simple. Because my husband was an anti-revolutionary, all I had to do was go down to the Party office, sign a paper of divorce and my marriage would be over. He came to me and pleaded, 'Marry me. Be a part of the Revolution. You can come and live in my home and bring your children with you. I will give you clothes and I will give you food.'

"He'd come late at night and knock on my door to visit me. He would come into my house and he'd say, 'Divorce your husband. All you have to do is sign this paper and your marriage is over. He's an anti-revolutionary. He'll be gone for twenty years. You'll never hear from him again. You cannot write to him. He cannot write to you. What does it matter?' I told him, 'I am a Christian. Christians do not believe in divorce. I am married to my husband.' 'What about if he's dead?' he'd ask. 'Then you would be free.' I realized that this high Party member could arrange my husband's death. What was one more body in the great scrap heap of history that Chairman Mao was creating? 'No,' I told him, 'I married my husband forever. I don't need a letter from him for me to still love him, for I have a letter from the Lord, not from man.' Finally he gave up. And the children praised the Lord with me. I did not betray their father and make them live with this awful man. I would not divorce my husband."

Well, twenty-two years have passed with pressures exerted again and again in varying forms. But the power of God triumphed. One day Mao Zedong died and things changed. There was a reunion: a faithful husband, a faithful wife and the children now grown.

As the interview ended, they said they had a song they used to sing even when they were apart. They held hands like newlyweds and began to sing for us in that room.

Together, each held up his or her half of the sky.

Millions gather in Tiananmen Square to
mourn Mao's death in 1976.

Though the police watch house church activities, the sheer number of people attending each service makes control nearly impossible.

Often, as with this house church, there is standing room only.

Evangelist Billy Graham, whose wife Ruth was a "missionary kid" in China, preaches at the church led by Pastor Lamb.

An itinerant evangelist prepares to end a nine-hour teaching session.

David Wang says good-bye after finishing a three-day "Bible School in the Wilderness."

During a session of the "Bible School in the Wilderness," leaders study, sleep and eat in small rooms, and none venture outside.

After they themselves have been taught, Lao Da hold training sessions for the Lao Er.

After three days of prayer and fasting, "donkeys" from four different countries wait for the train to take them and their precious cargo to hands that wait in the North.

During the Cultural Revolution, young people attend a teaching session about Mao. Today, young people are openly taught about Jesus Christ.

Children in Beijing read Bible stories presented in cartoon form.

Children have always been at the heart of China's families.

For every couple engaged to be married, the joy of engagement is overshadowed by the government's mandated "one-child policy," which allows only one child per family.

Though social pressure is heavy, many Christian couples do not abort baby girls. These dear faces belie the pain that their parents went through in order for them to be born.

"Bible Women" in China truly do hold up their "one half of the sky," along with the men. One of these godly women cherises a Bible that survived the Cultural Revolution.

10

A MIGHTY VOICE

"Give the winds a mighty voice, Jesus saves, Jesus Saves . . ."
—*Priscilla Owens*

It has been half a century since Dr. Robert Bowman sat down at a microphone in Manila and told the people of China, "This is the Chinese service of the Far East Broadcasting Company, broadcasting from Manila, Philippines." He then played the first line of the last verse of a missionary hymn that was to become FEBC's signature: "Give the winds a mighty voice, Jesus saves, Jesus saves." Bob Bowman then turned the microphone over to an American missionary who had recently been expelled from China.

Today, as many as 380,000 hours of programs, in all major languages of China, have penetrated every barrier that man could construct. The people of China hid under blankets and in closets, risking prison and sometimes even death, for what was then a "crime against the State" and a severe "anti-revolutionary" act. They did so in order to hear God's Word: encouraging, admonishing, but most of all hugging an oppressed people to His bosom, reminding them that He tasted the salt of the tears caused by their persecution.

Though the Chinese government still forbids its people to listen to foreign radio broadcasts and classifies that as a crime against the State that will be severely dealt with, it is basically an unenforced threat. People no longer have to listen in secret. Though there are isolated cases of individual cadre leaders arresting house church leaders for violating the law, listening to foreign radio broadcasts is an accepted fact of life. When it is enforced, the punishment is usually no more than a warning. The introduction of the transistor radio made enforcing compliance impossible.

Although several other organizations broadcast into China, FEBC, under its Chinese Program Director, Kenneth Lo, still remains the primary provider. It has thirty-five and a half hours a day of programs transmitted not only from the Philippines, but also from South Korea and Saipan.

FEBC's 250,000 watt AM station in Korea remains a powerful voice into the population center off the central and coastal areas of China. Its signal is often stronger than that of local government stations.

There are two things that have changed, however: program response and program content.

There was a time when FEBC went seven years without one letter of response from China. Day after day, month after month, programmers continued their broadcasts in total faith that people were listening. Personal surveys of believers in China would later verify the significant role that radio played in the survival and in the building of what is today the largest body of believers in history, but there was no way to know that at the time.

However, in 1995, FEBC received 21,631 letters from China, plus 1,473 faxes. Non-Christians sent 6,447 of those responses, requesting more information about the subject matter of the broadcast. That translates into spiritual inquiry.

Before and after the Cultural Revolution, nearly all the programs centered on one great question: How does one survive under persecution? The word went out: "Don't give up; the world is praying for you." The Bible was read at dictation speed. Copies of those dictated Scriptures are still used in some house churches today. The person of Jesus Christ is still the central focus of all FEBC programs, but now the emphasis of the teaching is on evangelism, discipleship, and church planting in the Chinese context. The Bible Seminary of the Air receives the greatest number of inquiries from both Christians and non-Christians.

Samplings of the responses to the programs are indicative of the needs and aspirations of the Church in China. One listener wrote:

> "I have big trouble with my wife, who was once a believer but left God since her parents passed away. She always disturbs me and yells at me when I want to pray or sing hymns with you and your preachers. She once took some of the precious spiritual booklets that you sent me, as well as my Bible, and tore them all to pieces."

Another writes:

> "I am in great distress. My husband wants to divorce me. He strongly opposes my being a Christian. Sometimes when I get home late from a house meeting he locks the door and will not let me in and leaves me outside all night, all alone. In an outburst of temper he has torn my Bible to pieces and smashed the radio—it was my church, my preacher! Please pray for me."

Other letters give subtle indications that China still has a long way to go before it grants in actuality the freedom of religion stated in its constitution. Another listener writes:

> "We do enjoy our limited religious freedom. Officials pay much attention to our religious activ-

ities. Pastors' families are always being visited secretly by the police. Take myself, for example. When I was not at home, some people pretending to be believers came to visit my family members and questioned them about our occupation and our overseas friends. You know that those under 18 are not allowed to believe in any religion or, as they call it, superstition, and they cannot go to church. Churches are also forbidden to run Sunday schools that might influence children and youth. But don't worry, I won't give up. If God is for us, who can be against us?"

A surprising number of letters come from young people who are not supposed to participate in religious activities. A sampling of letters indicates why the government is nervous about the inheritors of Tiananmen Square.

"One day back in 1987 I tuned into your station by chance. I was then 18 years old and did not know Jesus. Then, after four years of college education, I deeply tasted the feeling of loneliness, emptiness and anguish. This year I, again by chance, listened to your program. I heard God calling to me. I found that God has been loving and caring for me. I felt the deepest gratitude in my heart, but also shame for my sins. Selfishness, jealousy, greediness, cheating, unforgiving and vanity are no big deal on the earth but are really sins in God's eyes. I realized that that's why my life has been a burden to me. I had been a slave of Satan. Because of you, I came to know Jesus Christ. I confessed my sins and asked for His forgiveness. I thank God for His blessing."

Another man and his wife, Cephas and Mary, were born and raised in Christian families inside China. During the 1949 Liberation, both witnessed the confiscation of their families' properties, businesses and belongings. Their parents were severely persecuted, particularly Cephas', since his father had relatives who escaped to Taiwan. The family was labeled pro-Nationalist. During every new political upheaval and movement, his father would be dragged out to the public square to be "struggled against." Finally, in 1967, he saw his father beaten to death by a mob of youngsters as a part of the Cultural Revolution.

"I remember two things about that day," Cephas said, "my father's dying prayers as he whispered, 'Jesus, save me . . . Jesus save me . . .,' and my vow to revenge this madness, this insanity of the leaders of my country."

Cephas then escaped to Hong Kong. He had been trained as an actor in China, so a commercial radio station in Hong Kong soon recruited him to do drama broadcasts. He met his wife, who had also escaped from China. She was also in broadcasting, working for a gospel station, producing and broadcasting the Good News to the children and young people of China.

"What do you tell them?" Cephas wanted to know.

Mary told him that she told her audience that Jesus loves them and that He alone can save them. Cephas knew, then and there, that broadcasting that message was to be his life's work: "I remembered my father's last prayer, and I remembered my vow to get back. The only way to get back is to tell the people in China of the love and salvation of Jesus."

Cephas and Mary have now been broadcasting that message for more than a quarter of a century.

The first time Cephas returned to his home town, he did not let anyone know what he was doing in Hong Kong. But again and again, house church Christians asked him to convey their heart-felt gratitude to the people in Hong Kong who beamed "the voice of heaven" into China every night. A group of believers told him that they got down on their knees as they listened to "Streams in the Desert" broadcasts, one of the longest-running gospel programs on FEBC.

Cephas and Mary also recall their visit to a faraway town on the northern border of China. "We met a group of young believers and when they learned that we were the voices in the gospel broadcasts, they cried and called us 'Papa' and 'Mama,' for they considered us as having given birth to their new life in Jesus."

Multiply these few examples by 21,631—the number of letters received in 1995—and you will have a little understanding of how important it is to continue to help give the winds a mighty voice. Millions are reminded daily, as they pluck that voice out of the atmosphere, that "Jesus saves, Jesus saves."

11

DONKEYS
FOR THE LORD

"See, your King comes to you, gentle and riding on a donkey."
—Zechariah

They sat together in a small room on the border of the Middle Kingdom. They came from seven different nations. Their languages and cultures were as diverse as their backgrounds. But none of that mattered. Diversities were made irrelevant by their mutual commitment to a single task. They were "donkeys." Their task was to carry a precious cargo to brothers and sisters in China, a cargo that all Chinese Christians long to hold, to study, and to call their own—Bibles.

It was illegal to accept foreign literature, especially from a foreigner. However, the recipients waiting inside China were willing to take any risk necessary to receive a Bible.

Quietly, the diverse group of carriers, ranging from teenagers to a grandmother, shared with each other the results of their latest trips. Some had gotten through and delivered their load, but some had not.

Who are these "donkeys," so loved by those to whom they carry that precious cargo?

One was born the youngest of three daughters. She was raised on a dairy farm in Australia, and all she really ever wanted to do was "take over the farm when Daddy dies." She knew she didn't have to study too hard at school to be a dairy farmer, so she spent time with the cows rather than the books. Her teacher wrote a note: "Your daughter would do better in school if she would hand in some of her written work." She was fifteen years old, expecting her dairy dreams to be realized in just a few years. Then, one day, all those dreams were shattered.

Her father announced that he had sold the dairy farm. "I was angry at my daddy, but more angry with God. How could He strip away my future?" She spent the rest of her high school days living in rebellion. She refused to turn in written assignments, high school sports and alcohol consumed her days and nights. "I reached bottom. One Saturday night I lay drunk on the floor, asking myself, 'What is life all about?' I cried out to God saying, 'Help me . . . please help me.' A simple voice spoke in my mind, 'If you continue this way, it will be your death.'

"I grew to recognize that voice as the voice of God. I still hear it, but now it does not frighten me.

"I used to hate my daddy, but one night God filled my heart with a love for him that I didn't think possible. I went to him, sat on his lap, and with tears rolling down my face, I was able to tell him I loved him. A few weeks before, I couldn't stand to be in the same room with the man who had betrayed my future, but since that day I have loved him with a very special love."

Two years later, she found herself in Bible college. It was there that she first heard about world missions.

The Dean saw potential in this young, spiritually vital girl. He asked if she would like to "go north and visit some Asians."

"No way," she answered. "I don't like Asians."

Before she knew it, she found herself crying out to God to give her compassion for those Asians.

Eight weeks later she arrived at the Donkey House, on the border of a nation with more than 1 billion Asians. But it was all right because God had performed another miracle in her life, and again her heart was filled with a love she didn't think possible. This time, it was a love for 1.2 billion Chinese. After several days of training, prayer and fasting, she found herself with an overloaded backpack, ready to walk across an international boundary into China.

She tried to remember what she had been told about customs officers: "Customs agents are not your enemies. They are just men and women like you doing their job. Part of that job is to make sure you don't take any Bibles across." She saw two lines forming. Her party of four split up so they would not look so obvious. She looked at each custom agent.

That one looks kinder than the one over there, so I'll get in this line, she thought. *Maybe he's a Christian.* Then she remembered that she was only a "donkey" and it was God's responsibility to make sure the cargo made it through. Donkeys are supposed to be dumb, so she acted dumb, too.

She jumped in a line and waited. Though she was sure she was on a divine assignment, her knees turned to jelly. She wished war would instantly break out between the U.S. and China so she could turn around and go home. Her mouth got dry. "Act normally," she had been told. "They will probably be watching you through two-way mirrors. They will notice you if you are too nervous."

Wait, she told herself. *God is in control here, not someone behind a two-way mirror.*

Her turn came. *Remember, never tell a lie. Just pray that the customs agent won't ask the wrong question.*

He may not be my enemy, she thought, *but he sure doesn't look like someone I could call "friend."*

"Are you carrying anything that you should not be carrying?"

"No."

"Where are you going?"

"To Guangzhou."

"Are you just a tourist?"

"Yes, just a tourist."

"Will you take your backpack off, please, and place it on the X-ray?"

Time stopped for her as she remembered a story told by the director of the program:

"There were these two young guys from Europe. They were instructed to pray for two hours and fifty-five minutes, and then to take five minutes to pack the cargo. They did just the opposite. They hid Scripture in their empty toothpaste boxes, inside books, inside their underwear. Every Bible was wrapped in a sock or a T-shirt. There was one problem; they never made it through. They were always caught. After three attempts, their supervisor told them, 'Now you are going to do it our way. I will send you one more time. You will spend two hours and fifty-five minutes praying, and five minutes putting Bibles in your backpacks. Be ready to leave tomorrow morning.' They followed his advice this time and the customs official waved them through. Many trips later, they have not been turned back since."

The young woman was glad she was prayed up. She had had more than two hours of prayer and, of course, a bit more than five minutes to pack. After all, she was a girl!

Too late to run, Lord. I'm glad this is your backpack, and not mine.

As the backpack slowly made its way through the machine, she heard a customs agent briskly speak to one of her fellow "donkeys."

"Young lady," he said to the second woman, "I asked you if you had any Bibles and you said 'no.' I am sure you know the Bibles in your backpack tell you not to lie, but you lied. Shame on you." He then wrote out and gave her a receipt for the Bibles and told her she could pick them up when she was ready to leave the country. "Next."

The first woman was startled as her agent pointed to her backpack and motioned her to continue on her way. "Thank you very much," he said. "Welcome to China."

She had made it! As she hoisted her pack onto her back, she slowly began her walk into China. Tears welled up in her eyes as she realized that she had done it. *No, I didn't do it. God did it. Out of the four of us, only one lost their cargo.* Once again, she heard that still, small voice: "Well done; you did a good job."

There would be other trips in the days ahead, and not all would go as well.

"Take a seat," the man was told. "It will take us a while to find." This was the response he received as he handed the hotel staff member a storage slip so he could pick up bags left there weeks before. Some time later, they returned with the bags.

"Do these belong to you?" one of them asked.

"Yes," he responded. Within seconds he and his teammate were surrounded by the local PSB (Public Security Bureau).

One word ran through his mind—busted!

After taking passport details and confiscating their bags, the two men were escorted back to their hotel, grateful to still have their toes and fingernails still in place, and to have saved the money they would have spent on a taxi. During the ride they chatted with Rose, the PSB officer in charge of the investigation. They asked her if she had ever read the Bible.

"Yes, I have one Chinese Bible and two English Bibles. I read them when I was studying in Beijing." Rose left them at the hotel.

They couldn't continue on their journey with their books, yet the opportunity to speak with Rose was one for which they were grateful. They prayed that she would be challenged to read her Bible and not see a Western god, but Jesus himself, who came to give hope and abundant life.

A woman leaned back in her chair, rehearsing the instructions from training. She had been in China for ten days, ninety hours on the train, delivering a load of literature. She and her team member, who did not like Chinese food, had already been to the same city twice.

There were fifty-three more hours on the train across a barren landscape. In the chill of dawn, the train grunted to a halt at their destination—a city empty and lifeless, no bigger than a country town. Outside the station, the first load of Bibles disappeared into the hands of waiting Christians.

After a few hours sleep, the team of five headed back to Beijing to pick up a second load. Then, leaving Beijing's bright lights, they endured eighteen more hours of the stench that always lingers in a filthy train carriage, and they went back to the same little city.

They struggled up and down the station steps with the heavy, loaded bags, while the eyes of the locals watched every move. As before, God's hand of protection was over them, and their second delivery was completed.

"Later that day we talked with the Christians we'd traveled so far to help. A young guy in his early 30s did all the talking . I listened intensely as he spoke of great revival—20,000 new Christians during Chinese New Year and thousands baptized over the past few weeks. He himself bore fresh scars from cigarette burns on his body, reflecting the persecution that still goes on."

Though the details vary, as these "donkeys" tell their stories, one senses a fulfillment of the words in those Bibles they carry: "Follow me. Don't run ahead, just follow in obedience."

Another man had been an associate pastor of a church in the United States. His wife and he had resisted getting involved in foreign missions, but finally, he could no longer ignore the inner urging from God. They agreed to a short-term commitment.

Several miracles verified that God had divinely led his wife and him. They had asked the Lord to do three things for them while on the mission field: 1) Strengthen their marriage; 2) Gain them acceptance in another culture; and 3) Help them learn some of the language.

God had provided the necessary finances and a leave of absence from their church. But now a decision had to be made. Their pastor back home had promised to hold the man's job and their apartment for one year. That year was up and it was time to go home. He had done his "missionary stint."

Privately, he wrestled with the Lord because the Director of the "Donkey Mission" had asked him if he and his wife would become on-site directors. That was a two-year assignment. As the struggle inside continued, he tried to pray it through logically. He thought of the good job and the security awaiting him at home. Then he remembered the faces of the Chinese brothers and sisters as they received the cargo he helped deliver. These people were not just stopping by a Christian bookstore to buy a "how-to" book. Some had traveled days in order to obtain just one copy of the Bible. Others had risked the wrath of the authorities. Many said, "You left your country to bring this to me! God bless you."

One morning the wrestling match was over. He told God, his wife, and anyone that cared to listen, "I don't care if I lose my job, our apartment, or our new car. We can forget our comfort zone. Our ministry is here." The burden that had been so heavy on his heart was lifted and smothered by the embrace of his wife. "I feel the same way, but I wanted God to be the one to convince you," she said through her tears.

"Our marriage and love for one another has been strengthened. I have been named director, and soon I begin language study."

As for their cultural differences, the Book that these two "donkeys" carried so faithfully to the Chinese believers taught them that in Christ there are no Chinese, or African-Americans or Europeans—only brothers and sisters in Christ.

Before the "donkeys" retired to their crowded quarters, some one told this story of an old Anglican vicar, retired from the ministry:

For years, the vicar felt his ministry had been a failure. Then he heard that he could carry Bibles to believers in China. He withdrew his savings and, along with his small pension, headed for Hong Kong.

The day finally arrived for him to take his first trip. It was a hot August. He attempted to hoist the pack onto his back and almost fainted. He was too weak from heat exhaustion to carry anything—let alone a backpack full of Scriptures.

The team had to leave without him. He sat and reproved himself for his continued failure. One of the young "donkeys" came by and began to talk to him, "I got caught and they stamped my passport so I can't get into China anymore, but I can still pray. Can you?"

"Yes, indeed. That I can do." And so the vicar prayed.

Later, he stood before those who had delivered the priceless cargo and returned without casualty:

"I started to pray for you young folks. I have spent a lifetime reading prayers and saying prayers, but this was different. I was being prompted by something I had never felt before. Soon I was not only standing, I was doing something I had never done before. It would not have been proper, or so I thought. I was weeping and then my hands went up in the air. Those hands seemed to separate the clouds, and I saw someone else praying for you wonderful people—my Lord Jesus Christ. You see, I may be too old to carry those Bibles on my back, but with His help I can carry you all on my back with my prayers."

He never got within fifteen miles of the Chinese border, but because of his prayers, many others crossed it—safely.

The argument still continues in some quarters as to whether or not it is proper to "smuggle" Bibles into China. A similar argument was heard in 1981. At that time, several of us wondered how those who wanted to receive a Bible felt about it. Their responses are still relevant today, and many more believers echo them.

"It is easy for those of you sitting at a feast to moralize about how to feed those who have no food and are starving."

"I have 3,000 people in house churches that I visit and teach. They have three complete Bibles and two New Testaments between them. What would you do if someone offered you a chance to get a Bible?"

"Let us decide if there is any danger involved. We can handle it. You just get the Bible to us."

"Let us take the responsibility before the Lord as to whether it is moral or not."

"Are we to tear out of the New Testament everything that Paul wrote? No! Well, don't forget that everything Paul wrote and did for the Church was done after the synagogue leaders wanted to kill him, and the believers smuggled him out of the city. Was that immoral?"

"When someone puts out an empty hand for God's Word, would you put a serpent in it?"

The need for Bibles continues to be critical. Though Three Self's AMITY Press has been granted permission to print a million Bibles a year, that is still not many when measured against the number of Bibles that are now available, the size of the Church, and the total population of more than 1 billion.

A poem by H.E. Fosdick helps give us some perspective.

I saw the conquerors riding by
     With cruel lips and faces wan:
Musing on kingdoms sacked and burned
     There rode the Mongol Genghis Khan;
And Alexander, like a god,
     Who sought to weld the world in one:
And Caesar with his laurel wreath;
     And like a thing from Hell, the Hun;
And, leading like a star, the van,
     Heedless of upstretched arm and groan,
Inscrutable Napoleon went,
     Dreaming of Empire, and alone . . .
(To that we can also add the names of Hitler, Stalin and
     Mao)
Then all they perished from the earth,
     As fleeting shadows from a glass,
And, conquering down the centuries,
     Came Christ the Swordless on an ass.

12

TENTMAKERS

"By trade they were tentmakers."
—*Luke*

Is China open to missionaries? The answer to this oft-asked question is yes; it is—but not in the traditional sense. "Tentmakers" are welcome—we call them English teachers.

They are part of an interesting osmosis that started in the 1980s when realism overshadowed Party rhetoric. China realized that if it were to join the family of nations, even if only to gain lost territories and world markets, they would have to do more than drink tea. The people would have to speak English. The call went out, and the first to respond were what the Chinese now call "pinkies." They came from Western university campuses, Mao worshippers, honed in the hallowed halls of Harvard and other similar institutions. As others had done decades earlier, they pronounced Stalinism as the "wave of the future," and saw Mao as the tsunami that would soon sweep over the world. Having never been closer to a prison than an anti-death penalty demonstration, having never had more dialogue with an unfriendly police officer than what it takes to get a DUI ticket signed after a fraternity party, they headed starry-eyed for the promised land.

They soon realized they had made the same mistake as Mao. They believed what the Western press and intelligentsia had said about his "great" ideals, and their being the wave of the future. Before long, both were dead and buried.

Disillusioned, the "pinkies" returned to where they came from, picked up their degrees, and headed for tenure. Over steaming cups of espresso in fancy coffee houses, they could solve the problems of the world rather than by listening, over steaming bowls of green gruel, to the litany of suffering from someone who was subjected to Mao's great experiment.

In the mid-1980s the Church caught the vision. Whenever new territory is opened, whether it is geographical or spiritual, pioneers must blaze the trail. English teachers from the United States were among the pioneers, following in the footsteps of their forefathers—the ones who had spread their way across open plains. Motives varied, but all, whether led by their own desires or by the desire of another, wanted to be part of an exciting adventure. Just as the American pioneers sometimes showed open disdain for those who had been in the land hundreds of years before them, these pioneers were unruly at times, but they were also courageous. Marginal in their cultural understanding but reckless in the initiation of their job, they had a tendency to shoot from the hip. They went where no one had been, and they did what no one had been able to do; they did their job and they did it well. They opened the frontier for the next contingent, the settlers.

Settlers brought to China the desire to build something permanent. They brought a law and order to their work. They were interested in long-term commitment. They believed in being well trained, disciplined and patient. Their desire was to live in the new territory.

Once the lands had been explored and settled, they realized China was ready for the next stage: the developers—those who would understand cultural sensitivities, were willing to make adjustments, doing things within the framework of what had been done for thousands of years. Where the pioneers were reckless, and the settlers too conservative, the developers took over and blended the best of both—and they truly "settled" the land. The pioneers and the settlers did what they went to do well. Without their work, the stage could not have been set for the developers. China now welcomes developers who love the Chinese— "tentmakers" like Jane and Lydia.

Jane and Lydia walked into the mission organization's office in Hong Kong the third day after the Tiananmen Massacre of June 1989. They collapsed and cried like babies. The emotional strain had built up until it had become too much to bear.

Four years before, they had gone to the capital city of China to teach English to the "future leaders" of the New China in response to an invitation from the mission organization. During their stay in Beijing, they had been visited on a regular basis with deliveries of practical supplies, especially both physical and spiritual food. They were now requesting large quantities of English/Chinese bilingual New Testaments. Many of their students were children of high-ranking officials—students who were disillusioned with the Party and with Communism as an ideology. They were now open to the gospel.

Quite a number of students from the university where Jane and Lydia taught participated in the Tiananmen Square democracy movement. Two students had been killed on that fatal night in June, and three were still missing.

Two days later, the two English teachers were "evacuated" by their consulate. Through tears of frustration they told their story:

"They came to our university in their diplomatic car to take us to the airport and told us to leave immediately. They said China was in such chaos that it would be in our best interests and safety to get to Hong Kong as soon as possible. We didn't want to leave because we love our students so much and we have begun to bond with many of them.

"One of the students killed was from our department. He was so bright, so energetic and full of hope. He often stayed up late with us, discussing philosophy or debating Christianity with us in his exceptionally good English. He studied the Bible and underlined passage after passage. He told us he thought he was becoming a believer of Jesus, but he was having a hard time validating the miraculous in His life. 'That takes faith, eh? Like the faith that brings you to China?' He even teased us."

The two tentmakers went to a Christian retreat center in Hong Kong for rest and recuperation. Less than a week later they returned to the office with airline tickets in their hands, saying they were returning to Beijing the following day. "We know the situation is still most unstable. The consulate here told us that they would not be responsible for us if we go back to Beijing. But we have no choice. We have developed a relationship with out students. They need us now. We also need them to bring healing to us."

Kathy was another tentmaker. She was 26 years old when she first heard the name Liuzhou. She hadn't read it in any book or magazine. She did not hear it from anyone. But one night, after she completed correcting the homework of her students and was preparing to retire for the night, she heard God.

"It was as clear as a bell that He wanted me to go to Liuzhou to teach Chinese students," she said.

Kathy had never considered being a missionary, and she was not prepared to leave her quiet, quaint town on the South Island of New Zealand. But God spoke to her again: "I am sending you to Liuzhou to teach the Chinese English, and through your life, they are to learn about my love."

A few days later, Kathy had a map of China and found the

city, located on China's southern coast. She took a trip there during her school break, all by herself, without any references. "If it was really God who wanted to send me there," she explained, "He would have to open the doors. I would not tell anyone of this 'message' from God, either. He would have to provide the finances and everything."

Kathy put God to the test. The first big building she saw in Liuzhou looked like a school. She walked in and introduced herself to the principal. When he finally understood what Kathy was saying, he exclaimed with an accent Kathy could barely understand, "Your God must answer atheist's prayers as well. We have been looking for an English teacher. But our school is not large enough to approach the government to recruit an English teacher for us from abroad. I was at my wit's end, not knowing how we could get someone from outside. Where did you say you are from? South Island? Where is that?"

Two months later, Kathy obtained her papers to China. She moved into the dormitory with the local teachers and lived like the rest of the faculty. The school pays her a meager salary, but Kathy is totally content. Everyone in the school loves this country girl from New Zealand, and she loves everyone there as well. "I develop their English; they develop my obedience to my God."

The wife and children of the principal are now Christians, as are two other teachers and twenty-some young students in the school.

Yes, China is open to missionaries—if they come as tentmakers, ready to build something permanent for their Master.

13

PASSING ON
THE FAITH

"The things you have heard from me . . . these entrust to faithful men, who will be able to teach others also."
—Paul

Does China have Bible schools? Yes, and perhaps the most effective are found in the wilderness.

A young Chinese pastor in Hong Kong was sure that God had prepared him for something. He had taken advantage of all the special opportunities God had given him. He had absorbed the teachings of a godly mother, gained an education, was obedient to the voice of the Lord and now he was eager to be called. Through a friend, he made contact with an itinerant evangelist who traveled around the country preaching the gospel. After much persuasion and one of those miracles that he loved to expect, he was invited to join the evangelist as he traveled illegally around China. The pastor's first lesson was that the evangelist was, in many ways, a literalist. If Jesus said it, that was it. The evangelist knew that his job was not to argue but to go and do likewise. The two men carried no purse. Those they ministered to fed them, but the hosts' meager lifestyles did not permit them to do much more than that. The pastor and the evangelist rarely traveled with any food; rather, they depended on the Lord to supply it when they arrived at the next village. If it was too dangerous to stop in a village, they would just go on to the next village. Many nights they slept under the stars, where the evangelist taught the pastor the fine precepts of involuntary fasting, and voluntary prayer.

After two weeks, the young pastor, though greatly refreshed in spirit, had used up all of his physical reserves. "Why do you keep moving so fast?" he asked the evangelist. "Some of the people asked you to stay longer, but each morning before the sun is up you awaken me, and we walk together in the darkness, not sure where we are going, except we know that since this is China, there will always be another village just down the road. Sometimes that village is very far away. When the sun comes up, the days are as hot as the nights are cold."

Attempting to make a slight scratch on the serious veneer that the evangelist put on every question, the pastor tried a Western expression he had learned: "Relax man, you're too uptight . . . those villages will still be there tomorrow."

"You are right. The village will still be there tomorrow, but I am not sure I will still be. You see, my brother, what we are doing is illegal and the police are right behind us. I have not been home for four years. I have a family—two boys like you. They meet me once in awhile in one of the villages where their relatives live, but I know that if I go home I will be arrested."

The young pastor, frightened by the thought of the police right behind them was too embarrassed by the shallowness of his earlier speech to speak again. The evangelist sensed this, and for the first time did relax—but just for just a second. He spoke to the pastor as he would speak to one of own his sons during their infrequent times together: "You see, I cannot get arrested because I cannot afford the luxury of going to prison."

Three days later, while walking on the outskirts of yet another village, the evangelist put his arm on the shoulder of the young pastor: "I thank the Lord for allowing us to travel together. You have taught me many things. But now we will part company."

The young pastor looked at his mentor and asked, "Am I like Mark or Barnabas?"

The evangelist smiled, "See, you are beginning to think like an evangelist. But in praying about you, the Lord has told me that you are to have a different ministry. You are to be a teacher."

The young pastor turned and looked the evangelist in the face. "I?" he asked, full of incredulity and pointing to his chest. "I, who could hardly keep up with you, and who loudly complained? Worse, I was silently grumbling about being hungry and never being able to slow down. I did revive a bit when we would meet with fellow believers, but then I picked up my private whining where I left off as we went to the next village. Am I to teach you?"

"Yes. God has prepared you. You know things about the Lord that you have learned from His wonderful Book. You know and understand your Bible. Until last year I had never seen a Bible. Oh, I'd seen a few pages passed from one hand to another— Scriptures that had been faithfully transcribed on a piece of paper—but you have studied this wonderful Book. I am an evangelist. But often those I tell about Jesus follow Him for a short time and then they fall away, or someone with crazy ideas about the Lord leads them away. Our church needs to build a stronger foundation on what we believe and why we believe it. I hunger for more of God's Word. I have been secretly envious of your knowledge, but it would be selfish of me not to share you with others. In the next village we will meet with some leaders of the church. They will gather shortly after we arrive. They will want to ask you many questions."

Arriving in the village, there was little that distinguished the evangelist and his friend from the others in the small teahouse where they stopped. The lady who ran it knew everyone and was very friendly. She called them "strangers" and welcomed them to her village. The evangelist smiled and returned the greeting.

Halfway through drinking their tea, she walked by and stuck a piece of paper under the evangelist's teacup. He pretended not to notice, then he read it and crumpled it up in his fist. Suddenly he rose, announced that he had a very busy day ahead, and thanked her for her hospitality. He said he wished all the ladies in China could make such delicious tea. She acknowledged his gracious remarks, never looking up from pouring tea for four policemen.

As they stepped outside, the pastor breathed a great sigh of relief. "There were four policemen in there. They were not behind you. They were beside you at the next table!"

"Yes, I know one of them very well." He opened his fist and read the crumpled paper again. "Come, they are expecting us."

They walked silently down a street, past a small market. The street began to narrow so they could no longer walk side by side. The evangelist turned and spoke as they continued to walk, "Remember in school when the teachers would give you an examination? They would ask you many questions to find out whether or not you were worthy to be a teacher and to teach others what they had taught you?"

"Yes, it happened many times."

"Well, now you are about to have another such examination."

Before the young pastor could ask him what he meant, they came to an alleyway even narrower than the street through which they had just passed. They walked a few yards and the evangelist said, "This is it. I must go now."

"Go? Leave me here? Where are you going? When will you be back for me?"

"I do not know." He turned to leave. As he walked away, he looked over his shoulder and said one word: "Timothy." Then, he disappeared around the corner.

A door opened and an elderly man beckoned him in. This house, like all the other houses he had visited, was sparsely furnished. The bed and one of the tables were attached to the ceiling with ropes. With a few tugs of the ropes, the bed and other furniture could be lifted to the ceiling and the floor would then be clear for many people to sit. This was a house church. Five elderly men stood and greeted him as he came in. He felt very insignificant, as he was perhaps only one-third their age.

It didn't take long for the examination to begin:

"Tell us all you know about Jesus and the temptations."

"What would have happened had Jesus refused to suffer at Gethsemane?"

"When Moses blessed the tribes, why did he not bless the tribe of Simeon?"

Quietly and patiently, they waited for his answers. If he did not know he would simply say, "I am sorry, that is beyond my limited knowledge." They would nod, sometimes smiling at each other, and then the questions would continue. After many more questions, and as many cups of tea, one of the men began to thank him for coming and sharing his knowledge with such "simple-minded men." The others followed the elder's lead and stood to make similar comments. The pastor knew the examination was over, but he didn't know if he had passed or failed.

Several men took his hand and graciously invited him to come back and honor them with his presence, but set no date. They all nodded, but the pastor knew this was not really an invitation to return. It was simply Chinese hospitality that is so often misunderstood by the Westerner who thinks they really mean what they are saying. The door was opened and someone pointed to the alley, indicating it was time for him to leave. It was then he knew that he had failed the exam. He wasn't surprised. How could he teach these men who had survived many years in prison for their faith—faith gained through missionary teachers. They had been taught God's Word by His Spirit. They knew how to recognize heresy and how to avoid it. How could the evangelist ever have imagined that he, so young, could teach anything to these modern day Pauls?

Feeling more like the young Mark that Paul had chastised than the Timothy that Paul had praised, he turned to walk down the alley. Before the door closed, an old man shuffled out. Without looking up he said, "I know you are a very busy man with many responsibilities. You travel to foreign countries preaching and teaching." He paused as if to gain boldness to say what he wanted to say. He looked directly into the face of the young pastor and said, "Could you find a few precious days to come back and teach some of our leaders?" There was a pause and he interjected, "There would be more than there were today, and we will make all the arrangements."

"Me? Teach you?"

"No, He will do the teaching; you will be His vehicle."

A trembling, "Yes," was the only response he could muster.

"You will hear from us. God bless you." The old man turned and pointed to the end of the alley. "A young man will meet you there and escort you out to the bus station." The old man turned, quietly gave a nod, and closed the door behind him. The pastor stood alone. He had passed the exam, but was he really ready?

Back in Hong Kong, several visitors arrived with messages. Plans were made, dates were set, tickets were purchased. Now, three months, eleven days and a couple of hours since he passed the examination, he was ready for the next part of the test. An escort met him at the train station with a bicycle. It was a well-known city, with many of the homes hewn out of granite cliffs. As he pedaled through the streets, following his host at a discreet distance, he began to notice a sameness about the dwellings—small wooden structures blended into the rock cliffs that towered above. But this village was famous for more than its cliff dwellings. During the Cultural Revolution this village had become a model for the future. Its citizens had boasted that to live here was to live in the future. They proudly proclaimed, "Mao's great thoughts have banished poverty and sickness! All religion and superstition have been destroyed!"

Mao died and the village exploded, but not in the way many expected. The real reason there was no poverty or sickness was about to be revealed. Religion and "superstition" had not been banished; it had been nurtured. Though there was no ordained pastor in the village, there were suddenly twenty house churches. Led by a 31 year old farmer, that which had been boiling just below the surface was allowed to overflow into farmhouses, prisons and tea shops. The village now had 56,000 believers and was known as "that Christian village." The police and government officials paid particular attention to what went on in this village, but here it was not always to persecute, but to find out why the Christians were so different. When ambitious Beijing leaders wanted to clamp down on religious activities, the cadre leader reminded them that of all the villages, this one had very little crime and the people took care of each other. More importantly, the people had almost doubled the required quota in food production and manufactured products that Beijing and its officials depended on for their survival.

The pastor followed as his escort wove his bicycle down the street. He stopped, pointing to a house. It was built like the rest, up against the rock. The pastor leaned his bicycle against the small front of the house. This was the first meeting place of what would later be known as the Bible School in the Wilderness. It consisted of a three-day meeting with the *Lao Da,* the senior leaders of the house church movement, and a "visitor."

The pastor tapped on the door. It was immediately opened by an elderly woman who graciously smiled and stepped aside so that he could enter. He squinted as his eyes adjusted to the room. There was a bed on one side of the room, with a table and a couple of rickety chairs in the middle. Beside the bed was a stack of firewood, piled up against a stone wall. Sitting at the table was an older man. He stood and bowed slightly. The pastor recognized him as one of the men who had participated in his examination.

"Please sit down and we will have tea. All is ready."

After a few moments of discussion, this visiting pastor knew he was in the presence of two of God's special servants. The man was the pastor of a large local house church, numbering more than 800 people. The woman, who poured him some boiling tea, was his wife. He had heard about her. During the Cultural Revolution she would carry Mao's little red book in public. At home, she would dig out the Bible, which they had wrapped in rags and buried under the floor, so they could memorize Scripture together. They would cut out a page and re-bury the precious Book. After studying that page, they buried it in another place. If the police should break in when they were reading they would only get one page and not the whole Bible. Now, she traveled to other villages, singing what she had memorized—not verse by verse, but chapter by chapter.

The only sound in the room was the sipping of hot tea and an occasional "Praise the Lord" uttered under their breath as though it must be said confidentially.

Suddenly, without any prelude, the old man set his cup down, looked at the visiting pastor, smiled and said, "It is time." He removed several pieces of firewood from the bottom of the pile by the stove. The rest of them came sliding down. All that was visible was a dark hole carved in the stone. Then, he stepped back and motioned for the pastor to enter.

It is not uncommon for most of the small houses to have a room, hewn out of the rock, in which to store their vegetable harvest in preparation for long, severe winters. It was now spring and most of the vegetables had been eaten or shared with those who needed them. The visitor stooped to make his way through the small black opening.

"They are inside," the old man told him as he continued to move forward. A small shaft of light could be seen ahead. As he approached it, he could smell and feel the presence of other people. He lifted his head in surprise, knocking it on the top of the cave. In front of him, lit by one small light bulb, was a group of smiling faces. Several people stood, extending their hands. They led him to the only unoccupied place in the room, directly under the naked light bulb hanging from a stick propped against the stone wall. He sat on the floor, putting his bag containing his Bible and hymnal between his crossed legs.

"We are ready to begin. Let us thank Jesus for bringing us together," someone said.

During the prayer, the pastor looked around him, trying to adjust his eyes to the darkness. He could see nothing but uplifted faces and uplifted hands. After a long time of prayer, the senior *Lao Da* said, "Jesus has brought you here. Now share with us what He has told you to share."

For three days, from 5 a.m. to 11 p.m., forty-two brothers and sisters sat, listening intently, taking notes, and sometimes asking questions. Some leaned against the stone wall, but the visiting pastor had to remain seated. Quietly, one at a time, they took turns going behind a curtain to relieve themselves. Everyone studiously avoided noticing the sound—therefore, to the Chinese mind, it wasn't really happening. Twice a day, several young people brought plates of vegetables and hard, yellow corn buns. In the evening, the vegetables would be accompanied by hot soup that the visiting pastor was sure was intended to kill any germs that might come uninvited to the meeting. Chopsticks reached out and over each other as each picked up food and put it in the bowl he carried—the same bowl that would be filled with scalding soup in the evening.

While they ate, some kept questioning, and the pastor answered. If his mouth was full of vegetables, or if he was attempting to bite into a bun, the senior elder would answer for him.

Late in the evenings, the senior elder would start singing a song or he would pray, signaling the end of that day's teaching session. As the worship began, the visitor would have his first opportunity to lean back against the stone wall. The prayerful worship service was over when the last person was asleep. They slept leaning against each other or against the wall. As they woke early the next morning, they were eager to repeat the schedule of the previous day.

"It is wonderful in this cave," one person said. "We can sing and pray as loud as we want and no one can hear us." Others chimed in, pleased with the security of the arrangements that had taken months to prepare. One man leaned towards the visiting pastor and whispered, "Two of our brothers and one sister cannot be here. It is too dangerous for them, for they are being watched."

As a personal testimony was given, the senior leader whispered, "He has just been released from prison. He has been arrested many times. He told me that because the authorities know that he and his family are church leaders they follow him. He acts as a decoy. When we want to meet in one place, he leads them to another. He spends much time in prison but does not mind. He feels he can minister there as well as outside the prison. He believes the sinners in prison are no worse than those outside. The prisoners trust him because he was one of them. He sees many of his converts later in house meetings. He, too, says he likes to be in prison because it is so exciting to get out and notice how many have come to Jesus and are now worshippers. Though he lives not far from here, he walked more than a hundred miles over five days. If anyone was following him, they would have gotten too tired to continue."

The visitor heard of others, too, who had traveled for several days without food or money, and walked long distances out of the way in order to avoid police checkpoints.

A sister spoke of concerns that cults seemed to be growing in her region. The leader whispered, "She was recently imprisoned for nine months without a trial. They finally let her go. Her fellow believers got together enough money to bail her out, but she refused. She insisted on staying in jail and ministering there. She said the Lord does not make mistakes and jail was where He wanted her. Later we found out from some of the prisoners she led to Jesus that she had been tortured and severely humiliated. She will not talk about it, but simply says, 'It is an honor to carry on my body the marks of my Lord Jesus Christ.' She then changes the subject."

The visitor leaned forward and listened to her with renewed intensity. "Sometimes," she said with a hint of frustration, "we are like fire fighters, constantly called on to solve problems in our congregations." There was mumbled agreement from others in the cave. "The problems are most often in the new, first-generation Christians. They, like us, face all kinds of conflicts—personal, financial and political."

"Yes," another added, "and they also have problems with the authorities—some of whom not only harass them but claim to be fellow Christians in the other church—telling them that they would not have these problems if they would just join the Three Self. Then they would be taken care of and the officials would leave them alone, they say."

"I, too, have that problem," volunteered a young man, "but my greatest problem right now is the infiltration of false teaching of the cults which leads to heresy."

"That's right," said another, "and the government uses these heretics—like those who say we must shout or those who have to stand on their heads to pray—as an excuse to get rid of us because they say all Christians belong to the same superstitious sect."

"And do you note," added one of the sisters, "that these cult leaders appear from out of nowhere as soon as we begin to have a big revival? They are wolves, taking away the lambs."

Everyone stopped talking as the senior leader began to speak. "Ah, that is very true, but I would like to suggest that it would please our Lord if, instead of fighting cults and heresy, we give our energy to teaching truth, not only to them but to ourselves as well.

"Remember, brothers and sisters, the father of heresy is the devil and he is an egomaniac. He cannot stand to be in a place where he is ignored. We should not give him the satisfaction of distracting us from proclaiming the truth in order to fight heresy. To give him time is to lose some of our time to present Jesus. Let people hear the truth and they will make up their own minds. The Holy Spirit will not let His Word return void. Heresy is not so much a plague on our house as a push from God to intensify our preaching of the truth, as was the terrible persecution of Mao's Red Guards."

The sound of agreement followed by prayers for wisdom and guidance welled up in the cave. Wave upon wave of prayer bounced off the walls and ceiling in the rock, in an unnamed village in China, stoking the fires of a revival that would not burn itself out.

The visiting pastor knew that the future of the Church and all of China—perhaps even much of the world—would be determined by meetings such as this. He raised his hands to the Lord, and with tears of humility and thanksgiving added his voice to the great symphony. That must have sounded wonderful to the angels after the sounds of piteous whining they so often heard ascend from below.

The teaching resumed, along with questions and discussions of practical issues, as the sound of praying faded. There were no complaints, just realistic appraisals and requests for wisdom from the Lord on how to proceed.

"The harvest is so great," one said. "The laborers are so few. We need more shepherds."

"Yes, pray for me," asked another, "I am very tired. Not as tired as when I came, but I am constantly on the road traveling from village to village visiting my flocks. I am away from my family for more than ten months of the year. At that, I'm only visiting each church once every three or four months."

Each session ended with sage advice and words of encouragement laced with Scripture from a senior leader. Years of imprisonment and suffering had only strengthened his resolve to follow Jesus. These were the ones who had earned the right to speak.

"For many years," one man said, "my heart ached for fellowship and teaching such as this so we could know how to minister to the many thousands who are coming to our door saying, 'We want to see Jesus. We have heard He dwells here. Please tell us about Jesus.' Sure, brothers and sisters, we have problems, but they are the wonderful problems faced by Paul and Peter, not problems of Judas or Ananias and Sapphira. During the most difficult years, when my faith sometimes faltered and all I had was His word to repeat back to Him, I did not think I would see a day such as this. True, we are being watched, but why? Only because of Jesus. Yes, we are being persecuted, but why? Only because of

Jesus. We rarely see our family, and why?" "Only because of Jesus," the others answered altogether, like an anthem following a prayer.

He continued to exhort, and soon the anthem became a prayer of brokenness. These men and women had a commitment to Jesus Christ that shamed the visiting pastor, and his tears of humility were added to their cries for forgiveness. Through the sobs of brokenness came prayers that pride and selfishness be crucified on the cross.

Sometimes, the prayers of repentance continued for hours, but eventually the sobs and prayers would subside, and everyone would look to the visiting pastor for continued teaching. As he read from the Bible, others said the words with him as though they were reading too, although they had no Bible. He humbly taught with renewed strength and conviction, though he felt totally unqualified for the task.

Late on the third evening, as the moonless night turned black outside the cave, they began to sing and praise and pray together for the final time. One by one they tied their notebooks to their legs, under their clothes, or stuck them under their shirts as they quietly entered the dark night through the cave's tunnel. The visiting pastor continued to answer questions until only the senior leader remained with him. They, too, then stood and left the cave, leaning over. They paused by the wood pile.

When they were able to stand up in the house, the leader said, "You dropped an atomic bomb here. Like a great explosion, it has melted away many of our fears, and now we feel we are more than conquerors. Our fears have been replaced by His promises. The materials you gave us and the teaching of the Bible are the beginning of a great chain reaction for our church, and you will hear of many smaller bombs exploding." Opening the door, he said, "Go with Jesus. He brought you; He will deliver you back to your wife and children."

As the visiting pastor stepped into the cold dark air, the door closed behind him. He started walking in the direction from which he had come three days before. A young man on a bicycle quietly came alongside him. He dismounted the bike and indicated that the pastor was to get on it. As he mounted the bike, another man appeared on a bike to lead the way. The pastor was finally on his way home.

Later, on the long train ride, he could not sleep. What had happened over the last three days filled his whole being with fear, trepidation—and thanksgiving. The Lord had given him the privilege and responsibility of ministering, not just to thirty-six brothers and six sisters, but to church leaders of eleven provinces of China. Collectively, these leaders were responsible for overseeing flocks of more than 20 million Christians. The words of Jesus Christ ran through his mind: "Greater works than these shall you do . . ." like teaching His Word to shepherds of 20 million believers!

As the train raced through the darkness, he longed for the smell of boiled greens, scalding soup, and human sweat, and for the sounds of praise and worship. He dozed off singing, "There is a Redeemer . . ."

As the pastor's passport was being stamped at the Hong Kong border, the *Lao Da* were arriving back in their villages. As inconspicuously as they arrived, they let the second level of the house church, the *Lao Er,* know that they had very important information to pass along. After two and three day treks, the *Lao Er* begin to gather for seminars that will mirror to a large extent the one that was held in the cave.

These Chinese leadership seminars have no equivalent in the West. The participants wear the only clothes they own—a shirt and trousers, a jacket and shoes—often without socks. These are the same clothes they wear to preach—and to harvest their crops if they are farmers, to make bricks if they are bricklayers, or to sleep in as exhaustion overtakes them. It is not like a Western church conference, where the attendees sleep in nicely appointed rooms, showering before joining the rest of the participants at a buffet breakfast, where more food is served than a Chinese fellowship would consume in a week. They do not have to make tough decisions about which seminar to attend: How to Find God's Will, or How to Find Life after Divorce, or The Wounds of Spousal Abuse, or How Not to Be a Victim Again or How to Pray Effectively in Twelve Steps, or Is the Bible Inerrant, or What to Do When All Else Fails, or How to Double Your Church Membership in Just Twelve Months.

At these conferences, held in villages throughout China, the participants each bring a small bag containing a contribution of food for the four days, a Bible if he has one, and a notebook. These leaders each lead several congregations, preach in many pulpits, evangelize in new territories and nurture believers both young and old. By day they are farmers, carpenters, fishermen, teachers and factory workers. They receive no pay from their congregations. Some are so young that the Public Security Bureau Police ignore them, thinking them too young to have a significant position of leadership. Some are mothers with little children tied to their backs. No childcare is provided at this conference. These leaders are thrust into pastoral roles, almost to a person—because so many new Christians who are hungry to be fed look on them as "mature Christians."

Like their elders in the cave, they begin the four days of their conference at dawn, with prayers, praise and worship. Then the teaching sessions begin, followed by many questions and answers. Problems of theology, church organization and heresy are dealt with. The teaching leader's wisdom is recorded in their notebooks.

They sit for hours, shoulder to shoulder, knees pressed against the back of the people in front of them. Twice a day they take time for a bowl of rice. Not everyone can fit into the room, so some listen through a window. They have no covering from the hot sun, and those farthest from the window ask to have what they cannot hear repeated, and they then write it down.

One thing they do not do: they do not complain. They only praise the Lord for the opportunity to receive teaching and to have fellowship with co-workers. At night those who live close by go home and return in the morning. Some take others with them to spend the night in their homes. The rest sleep where they are, side by side, shoulder to shoulder. For the elder leader it is no different. Drained, exhausted at the end of the day, he leans back and sleeps on the floor. The next morning he will be one of the first to wake, sit up and start praying. The hot tea and bowl of rice will come later.

All over China, these illegal religious activities are taking place. Sometimes the police find out and there are arrests, but like their elders, these leaders do not allow themselves to be bailed out. They consider their prison terms part of their ministry.

Before the conference is over, there is a brief time for testimonies. One man shared the following:

"I am a 48 year old farmer. I till the soil from dawn to dusk, and then I go till another kind of soil and plant the seed." His gaunt figure, furrowed brow and swarthy skin speak of the weather-beaten existence. "I became a Christian in 1975 during my son's illness, but I knew little about Christianity because it was during the Cultural Revolution. I became truly born again in 1988. A year later a church came into existence in my village and I was chosen to be the leader because I had been a Christian the longest. I objected. I told them I am not even a graduate of primary school. What do I know? What I have learned I have taken down in this notebook from Christian radio broadcasts. I tried to take notes, but I missed much because of my limited knowledge of the Scripture and my small vocabulary. Then one day, a young tourist from another country came to our village. I stood watching him walk through the marketplace. I was wondering what he was thinking of China. I saw one of my friends speak to him, and then he turned slightly and looked at me. I just stood there.

"Slowly he made his way over to where I was standing, waiting for one of my children to finish buying vegetables. As the foreigner slipped his shopping bag into my hand, the kind of bag we all use for our marketing, I slipped him mine and I hoped this was my time of blessing. I had heard of such things. I dared not look into the bag. I hurried home and as soon as we were in the house I dug down into the bag the stranger had given me. Under a few vegetables, there was something wrapped in brown paper. My wife and children watched as I tore off the paper and held—for the first time in my life—a Bible. We all fell on our knees, crying and praising the Lord. Now I could preach. I had the Book."

As he held up the Book, many others in the room did the same. Each had his own story of how he became a pastor and how he got his Bible.

Once the conference was over, these leaders inconspicuously left the meeting place one by one. They returned to their villages, where they began passing word to the next level of the church leadership, the *Lao San:* "There is much wonderful information. There will be a meeting." The *Lao San* are often young and bold. One Christmas, they made a large sign that read, "JESUS CHRIST WAS BORN ON CHRISTMAS DAY. HE IS STILL HERE AS OUR SAVIOR." It hung in the village marketplace until the police removed it. Many of these young men and women bravely walk down the street carrying their Bibles to the meeting place. So many have been arrested that the police have backed off, unable to arrest them all.

These are the ones who will spread the message among the

people. They often are the new converts—some are older but many are young. The farmer will carry the message to other farmers, the shopkeeper to the customers, a student to other students and his teachers. These are the ones burning with what John referred to as "first love" in the book of Revelations. They are zealous and much more open than the *Lao Da* or *Lao Er*.

Their diaries record a fire similar to that recorded for us in the book of Acts: Ten brothers and sisters went to preach the gospel in the poorest areas. As soon as they started to preach, the power of God came down, causing the passers-by and street-sellers to stand still and listen. Even fortune-tellers were moved by the Holy Spirit and burst out crying. Many forgot to eat, to work, or to return home. This went on until evening, but still the crowd would not let them leave. The authorities then laid hands on them, beating them, but the revival continued.

Mao's army seemed defeated following the Long March, but it found its renewal in the caves of Yennan. In the same way, the Lord's army, seemingly defeated by the Cultural Revolution, continues its renewal today—in caves, in mountain villages, in parks, and in homes across China.

READINESS

Section Three

14

THE PLANS
OF GOD

"For I know the plans I have for you, plans for welfare and not for calamity, to give you a future and a hope."
—The Lord

"The miracles of the past are not sufficient for the problems of today," Abraham Lincoln said during America's Civil War. Those in the senior level of leadership in China's house church movement have a similar feeling. They know they must not live in the past, nor can they ignore it. At the same time, they are often thrown off stride by the rapidity of the events engulfing them.

They know that their survival and the survival of the Church is dependent on God and His plans. But they are disturbed by the fact that the new leadership will not have the same opportunities they have had to lay down their lives. There will be no long years of solitary confinement, no long separations from their families, while they wonder if they will ever see them alive again, and no running from city to city. In short, the crisis of the Church in China today is not suffering and persecution; it is one of little suffering, if at all.

To illustrate this fear, they will quote Pastor Wang Mingdao, one of their mentors. He is commonly acknowledged as the patriarch of the house church movement. Upon his release after twenty-seven years of imprisonment, he said, "Little brother, the book of Romans tells us that persecution and suffering cannot separate us from the love of Christ, whereas Revelation warns us that riches and comfort will cause us to lose our love for Christ."

The great burden of the elders can be identified in what they refer to as the "five crises that need to be overcome." There are nods of agreement and excited interjections as these are listed.

1. The Church is fast becoming traditional and mechanical.

"Yes, some of our believers are now meeting just for meeting's sake. There is less anticipation of God and more expectation from man," one leader said.

"I notice it too," another added. "We are fast becoming traditional. Our preachers and teachers are hearing less from God while speaking more about other things."

"True, true," another said. "Our revival fire is diminishing now that we have more liberty to meet."

Sadly, the elder of the elders rubbed his hands together, looked at the floor and added, "We used to meet whenever we could, and that meant almost every night people were meeting together to pray and to copy and study the Bible. But now, we are only meeting on Sundays—only one day a week. Our Lord must be very sad that we leave Him alone for six days."

2. Leadership is in transition and fatigued.

"Look at me. I can barely walk, but I am so busy that I hardly have time to spend the hours I need to study my Bible. I am traveling non-stop and I still do not have an assistant," one pastor said.

"Me as well," another agreed. "I have no assistant because I cannot find a younger one to go with me. They are too soft, and they don't want to go up the mountains or down to the villages. They want to travel by train or bus, so I guess I will just keep on walking until I can walk no more."

"I, too, told some of my younger ones this very thing, but they are no longer listening to me," a third man told the others.

"One of my young men told me, 'You old men are just hanging on to your persecution and suffering and you want us to endure the same, but these are new days for China.'"

"They are indeed that."

"It must be so sad for our Jesus to see this disunity."

"But they do not understand that all we want to do is get the job done. We want to see the work, if not completed, at least continued."

"I sent two to Bible school and they came back with nothing but criticism against me. They said, 'When you old ones meet with outside visitors from other provinces and foreign guests, you never introduce us to them.' I tried to explain that we are already exposed, but that we must not endanger them."

"Ah yes, I feel like a firefighter rushing about solving problems. I am very tired and need a rest, but I fear that our successors will not do well."

3. Division and distrust are gaining inroads fast.

"With the open door policy, everything from Coca-Cola to cocaine, from *Pilgrims Progress* to pornography, is finding its way into China, but how can we stop it?" a pastor asked.

"I have seen it in my churches," another continued. Something we never had to worry about before—denominationalism is coming so fast, causing conflict between pure evangelicalism and unbalanced charismatics."

"Yes, yes, only a short time ago we were known as the most charismatic church that did not know any of the Pentecostal labels, structured by Brethren tradition, standing on the Fundamentalists' Bible, High Anglican in Holy Communion, Straight Baptist in baptism, and like Girls' Brigade in our missionary force—a one-church Church. But, oh my, look at us now. Denominationalism is returning. All the labels are coming back."

4.   *There is a relentless onslaught of crude materialism.*

"Have you been to Shanghai lately? Skyscrapers shoot up from rice paddy fields, fish ponds are turning into freeways, old neighborhoods with a thousand-year history disappear overnight," a leader observed.

"And what is that creating? Inflation, corruption and crime."

"I saw in a foreign newspaper that a poll of 500 international firms and business people named China as the number one most corrupt country in Asia."

"Yes, for years the Communists spat in our faces and called us Jesus' parasites. Against that we could stand, but now materialism is stabbing us in the backs with its shiny, bright daggers, 'Money is god, money is god!'"

"All the young people want to say today is, 'Old man, look forward. Look forward!' But do you notice that in Chinese the two slogans sound exactly the same? 'Look money-ward! Look money-ward!'"

"Have you been to Guangzhou? Hong Kong businesses have set up thousands of factories. The workers are promised huge incentives and big bonuses to work on the Lord's Day—to work seven days a week, and into the evenings. My friend, Pastor

Samuel Lamb, told me recently, 'The test of a strong believer and a weak believer is no longer his willingness to go to prison. That was the old method. Now the test is simply this: Is he willing to come to church or does he go to work on Sunday?'"

"And all it is doing is giving us more money to buy things people don't need."

"Yes, but there is one more crisis that will destroy us if we don't resolve it . . ."

5. There is competition between "Thine is the Kingdom" and "My Empire."

"I met with three saintly old sisters recently," a pastor said. "I have known them for a long time. They have never held positions of any sort, but are each highly respected by Christians in both the house church movement and the Three Self. The three, crying tears of grief and sorrow, reported that leaders in their churches are now jockeying for power, for fame and for 'opportunities,' such as invitations to meet with foreigners, traveling abroad, or sending their children and relatives to study in the outside world.

"They think that the temptations today are ten times more powerful and deceitful than the worst days of the Cultural Revolution."

As suddenly as it began, the discussion ended—not with a groan of self-pity—but with a cry of victory: "But we have seen worse times. Our Lord Jesus Christ has not brought us this far to let us down now."

After several hours of praise and worship, they disbanded. Walking slowly, some even limping, they headed back to their villages. They think not so much of the five crises, but of one great promise: *I will build My Church, and the gates of hades shall not prevail against it.* Nor shall the gates of tradition, fatigue, division, distrust, materialism, or worldly power prevail.

There was one last word: "Our Lord Jesus Christ gave us the Spirit of God to destroy Maoism, and now we must be equally committed to Him as He gives us the power to destroy Me-ism."

Unlike so many people in the West, the house church leaders see a crisis as a gift from God to add muscle to their spiritual lives. Crises throw light on where we have been, where we are, and where we are going, and they encourage us to move on with Him so that He might honor us with an even greater crisis.

These leaders are also painfully aware that when a crisis comes and we ignore it, or try to solve it in our own strength, with our own schemes, intellect and power, we turn it into a disaster. That may succinctly point out what is too often the difference between the Church in China and the Church in the West.

The future of the Church in China is not shrouded in any great mystery. It is a body of believers placed in the hands of a group of old men. With what seems to be genetic stubbornness, they first frustrated, and then little by little, exposed Maoism for the cruel sham it was. These old men must now prepare to pass the mantle of leadership to a generation of sometimes "arrogant yuppies." This new generation may be "all" the Lord has, but He is God. He does know what He is doing, and He has done some miraculous things with a whole lot less—to which all of us can well attest.

15

LESSONS LEARNED

"As for you, you meant evil against me, but God meant it
for good in order to bring about this present result, to preserve
many people alive" —Joseph

As we begin to prepare for the future of China, there are several lessons we can take to heart concerning the Church.

Lesson 1. Man may mean to be evil, but God always means to bring good.

Joseph was cruelly sold into Egyptian slavery by his brothers. Such an outrage was inexcusable; however, God used Joseph's enslavement to fulfill His purposes with his people.

Cruel and godless men, through ensuing centuries, sold their brothers or their birthrights for little more than a bowl of pottage. However, whether we are talking about Sennacherib, Caiphas, Herod, Nero, Bloody Mary, Napoleon, Hitler, Stalin, Pol Pot, or Mao, God used them all as "saws and hammers in building His Church.

Isaiah told us God's plan:

> *Remember this, and be assured;*
> *Recall it to mind, you transgressors.*

Remember the former things long past,
For I am God, and there is no other;
I am God, and there is no one like Me,
Declaring the end from the beginning
And from ancient times things which have not been done,
Saying, "My purpose will be established,
And I will accomplish all My good pleasure";
Calling a bird of prey from the east,
The man of My purpose from a far country.
Truly I have spoken; truly I will bring it to pass.
I have planned it, surely I will do it. (Is. 46: 8-11)

God's ways are not man's ways. Joseph's words to his brothers are echoed by thousands of brothers and sisters to the perpetrators of their persecution, "You meant evil against me, but God meant it for good in order to bring about this present result."

In 1949, when Mao declared China a socialist state, he wanted to be more than the architect and contractor; he also wanted to be the messiah. He wanted everyone to speak his name in reverent tones, to thank him for the food on their tables (when there was food) and to worship him as the great savior of their nation. Every morning the nation woke to the tune of *The East is Red*, blasting from loudspeakers that hung throughout the cities on lamp posts and trees:

> The East is Red
> The Sun is Rising
> Emerging from China is Mao Zedong
> He brings happiness and blessings to the masses
> Hooray!
> He is the Great Savior of the People

It is no coincidence that the Christian Church in China was in deep trouble at that time. Modernism had taken root in the city's churches, heresy was rampant, and the Church was in need of a thorough cleansing. A think tank of the world's great church growth experts could never have come up with the plan God had for the cleansing of His temple. He used Mao to bring the Church back to its knees. Mao didn't plan it that way, nor did his followers, but God did. Many attempt to record history, but God makes history. And Mao, in the end, would be little more than another Herod in His hands.

Modernism was not the only stumbling block that the body of believers in China encountered in 1949. There were others, and Mao did for China what no missionary could do. Mao, and often the Church, did not realize that he was as much under God's control as was the Church committee—maybe even more so!

First, there was the matter of transportation. You can almost hear some of Mao's sycophants going to him between his many dalliances, and deferentially telling him that if he wanted everyone in China to worship him as the supreme leader, that message needed to reach the people. "But we have so few roads," they would explain.

It could have taken up to seven months for missionaries who lived far inland to reach their stations. The last weeks of their journey had to be taken on the backs of mules. The "roads" were often simply a precipice, not wide enough for a mule to turn around; if the person riding the mule fell off, no one ever heard from him again. The mule, unable to turn around, would continue and eventually arrive at the station, alone. If Mao's messengers and message were to reach the people of his country, building roads would be a necessity.

Mao believed everything the Western press said about him—that he could do anything. Being a ruthless dictatorship, a fact the press studiously avoided mentioning, had its advantages. Mao and socialism boasted of the absence of unemployment. There were millions of people—former soldiers, the riffraff of society, and victims of natural disasters such as droughts or floods—that were standing around, shifting from one foot to another. Mao gave them a gift—a pick and shovel. Before a person could say, "Up slackers, arise and go forth," or sing, "The east wind is rising over the west, and we shall win, for history is on our side," these former unemployed had extended the existing 75,000 kilometers of road to 189,000 kilometers. Today, that seven month trip can be made in less than a week, and in a train or bus—not only on the back of a mule.

Another obstacle that hampered the deification of Mao (and the expansion of the Church) was the divided kingdom. Previously, warlords ruled different sections of China with impunity. Mao took care of that problem with something more than impunity. He sent out a proclamation that there would be only one lord in China—Mao.

The nation was also divided by language. There were four races and fifty-seven tribes, with 300 major languages and more than a thousand dialects. To communicate a directive to such a nation would be an insurmountable task—even for Wycliffe.

Again, you can almost hear Mao's underlings pleading, "But Comrade, though we now have roads and can reach the corners of our country, we have to preach your gospel in so many languages. It will take a very long time. We cannot send messengers from one province to another because they do not speak the same language. The people will only laugh and pretend to understand. Even if they do understand, they pretend that they don't."

Mao had a plan. "No problem. People need jobs, education, and ration cards for food."

"Yes, wise Comrade."

"Tomorrow I will sign a decree that Mandarin is now the official language in all of China. All business transactions, education and public conversation will be in Mandarin."

"As you say, Comrade."

In a short period of time the gospel of Mao was being preached all across China—in just one language. For the first time in China's history, the people were unified. Another obstacle had been removed.

"But wise Comrade, if we are to print your red book full of your wise sayings for each of your blessed subjects, it will be so heavy. People will need a wheelbarrow to carry it. Our language, you must admit, was given to us by Confucian scholars to keep the peasants ignorant. There are 47,222 characters, which makes the Little Red Book a big book."

"No problem, unequal little comrade. I will sign a decree that, effective at once, the language will be simplified so that all Chinese can write it. Go and simplify the characters!"

And they did. Mao's "Little Red Book" was soon printed and distributed all across China with only 1,556 simplified characters. Another obstacle was gone.

Again they approached their supreme leader.

"You again?" he asked. "What now?"

"Pardon me, Comrade Chairman, we confiscated all paper in the country and have put the Little Red Book in many hands throughout your great nation, as you ordered. Now, when the million people gather in Tiananmen Square to celebrate your birthday they, with millions more in our cities and villages, will be able to hold aloft your mighty words and shout 'Long Live The Great Chairman Mao.'"

"So what's the problem?"

"Well, Comrade, after the celebration, I fear your words of wisdom will not be read."

"What!"

"Comrade, 94 percent of your grateful subjects are unable to read."

Another decree was issued: "Put up loudspeakers everywhere." This was followed by another campaign: "Illiteracy must be wiped out. Everyone must learn to read." Millions gathered in study groups and soon the statistics were nearly reversed. Today 87% of the Chinese population is literate and if there were any Little Red Books around, they would be able to read the simplified characters while riding down a paved road.

But the revolution was not yet complete, and God had a few more tasks for Mao.

"Supreme Comrade, I know you have not been feeling well, and I do not want to disturb your most noble presence while you are eating, but . . . well, we have a problem."

"Speak. I'll keep eating."

"You have declared yourself the supreme leader of our great nation, and truly you are. You have ordered people to bow towards you before eating . . . please, eat your food."

"I have, and they had better."

"Comrade, there are still those who go to the buildings of religion to worship another messiah: a Christ, and one called Buddha, and many others. The Christians have their crosses on steeples, the Muslims their crescents. They are reading your great writings, but they are also reading the Christian Bible, the Muslim Koran and other sacred books."

"Burn them. No, stupid comrade, not the Christians and

Muslims and Buddhists and Taoists and all those other superstitious pagans—burn their books! Get the young people who are memorizing my words to put on their red armbands and get busy. Give me some paper. I'll write a decree that all old and religious books, other than my sayings, will be destroyed at public burnings. All places of religious worship will be closed—turn them into granaries or warehouses."

The Red Guards carried out their orders with great exuberance; soon the only publicly recognized messiah was Mao, and the only book was his plagiarized proverbs. Evangelistic rallies celebrating Mao were held in cities, villages and courtyards. Mao's sayings were held aloft, and posters and signs proclaimed his greatness and glory. A people not used to displaying their emotions or innermost thoughts in public now stood and vied for prominence in confessing their "sins" toward their god, Mao. Mao even gave them this new word. Men and women wept tears of repentance for their "sins," beating their chest (clothing was too precious to be rent in grief).

Mao's specialists had tested, refined and proven the brainwashing techniques used on U.S. prisoners of war captured by the Chinese in Korea. What the Chinese troops had been able to do in Korea, Mao's Red Guards helped accomplish in China. They created an atmosphere of painful uneasiness and anxiety, and a sense that everything was out of control. Though the nation appeared to be unified, they were able to add a feeling of separation in the middle of the togetherness. No one could trust anyone else. Every night the nation attended compulsory rallies that lasted until the early hours of morning. Drained and fatigued, they had no energy left for anyone but Mao. According to design, they began asking themselves, "What am I doing here? What is life all about? Is this my future?" Life seemed so empty—pointless. And China was ready for conversion. God brought good out of what man had intended for evil.

Mao gave China everything the Romans and Greeks had given the New Testament Church 2,000 years before. History repeated itself, and God finished with Mao's hardened heart. Mao died, but did not rise again. His Little Red Book died with him, and he left behind a country prepared and ready for another gospel. God's people came out from their secret places of worship, cleansed and purified, ready to carry out their Master's Great Commission. Bibles that had been carefully buried suddenly appeared—faster than Mao's gospel disappeared. A Church of 900,000 Christians, corrupted with modernism and discord, today numbers 80 million believers who daily live out their faith in Jesus Christ, their Savior.

An itinerant pastor can now travel on paved roads, preaching in a common language to a people who know how to confess sin. From Mao, the people of China gained a new understanding of the concepts of "sin" and "repentance." They are a people of one Book and one Messiah. (They've adopted the term "believer," because "Christian" has come to be a cultural term applied to those who come from the West and have a big nose and round eyes.)

A second event that man meant for evil but God brought good out of was what we now know as the Tiananmen Square Massacre. As an American, I lived in Hong Kong in the same apartment building as David Wang during Mao's Cultural Revolution. With my usual keen perception, I, like many others, thought the end had come for China, that Mao and his Red Guards had destroyed the nation in a way that plagues, droughts and internal conflicts had not.

I met the Tiananmen Square Massacre with the same hand-wringing as I sat in a hotel room in Hong Kong, unable to obtain a visa to China. Several of us sat in front of a TV screen, in painful disbelief, as we watched tanks run over the bodies of students who tried to stop them. Troops opened fire on thousands of unsuspecting demonstrators who were demanding that the government become more democratic. Other tanks rolled over tents where many students had taken refuge or were sleeping. Soldiers with machine guns mounted on flatbed trucks indiscriminately swept the streets with deadly fire. The hospitals were soon overflowing with what Mao had called the "flowers of the revolution."

One eyewitness reported the following:

"Doctors reported that the soldiers used explosive bullets which made it very difficult for them to heal the victims. Later the soldiers even tried to prevent the doctors from treating the students. In the center of the square, soldiers of the 27th Army bulldozed the thousands of dead bodies into a heap. Helicopters hauled some away in plastic bags for mass cremation. They parked their trucks and tanks around piles of bodies so that passersby would not be able to see what they were doing—using tanks to flatten the dead corpses, and then stacking them up on iron racks for faster cremation.

"On the fifth day or so after the massacre, soldiers of the 38th Army came in, showing friendlier faces. They began clearing the debris and were busy scrubbing blood stains from the stony surface of the square.

"Newsmen from Hong Kong and others who were there estimate that 7,000 to 9,000 were killed on June 4th and 5th. The number of wounded, many of whom died in the hospital, numbered more than 10,000. Yet on June 5th the spokesman of the State Council of the People's Republic of China, Yuan Mu, announced that only twenty-three students died, but over 2,000 soldiers were dead or wounded! In a recent government report to Western newsmen, the Chinese government told the world that the soldiers did not kill even one student.

"Chinese people all over the world protested against this atrocity that was unprecedented in Chinese history, except for the

Nanjing massacre committed by Japanese soldiers during World War II. The people in Hong Kong held a black sit-in in Victoria Park. One of the staff at CCRC who took part said it was the largest funeral service she had ever attended. Hong Kong Protestant Christians held a meeting and marched in Victoria Park on June 5th. The Catholics held a large mass the following week. In Taiwan, the Chiang Kai Shek Memorial Park grounds were filled with several tens of thousands of university students from all over the island, to commemorate their dead counterparts in China. Christians in Taipei held an eight hour vigil of prayer and fasting on June 8th and another funeral service on Sunday, June 11th. I was also invited to take part in this mass meeting held in the Taipei New Park. Over 3,000 Christians turned out.

"Less than one week after the massacre, the Beijing government, headed by Deng Xiaoping (who ordered the massacre), Yang Shangkun (the President, who directed the massacre), and Li Peng (the Premier), began to arrest student leaders, intellectuals and workers who led the 49-day democracy movement (April 16 - June 4)."[1]

Some are still imprisoned.

Deng, like Mao, attempted to once again cleanse the revolution. This time the students were the instigators, not the perpetrators. But one thing was the same—what man meant for evil, God used for good.

As a U.S. citizen, I finally got my visa a year later and went to Beijing to join my colleague David. Five years earlier I had walked through the campus and no student dared to look at me. I was considered an enemy, but now they talked openly. One student shared the following:

"The day after the massacre, at the university we went into mourning. We were mourning for fellow students and professors we could not find, and some we have never seen since that terrible day. It was so painful to go to Tiananmen Square and find bodies of our close friends and carry them back to their families for burial.

"But," he continued, "the protest moved to the campus, but not in the way anyone expected. The massacre at the Square destroyed our last hope for the modernization movement. Suddenly there was a vacuum and we began to realize it was a spiritual revolution, not material or political. We needed something that no man could take away from us. We needed to believe in something that no tank could ever crush out of us. We stood at the crossroads of life and we remembered how many had suffered for their faith in Jesus Christ—though we did not believe in Him and thought the believers to be old and foolish. Now we were prepared to suffer, but not for Mao, or for Deng Xiaoping, but for something more than that. For nine years I fought the idea of becoming a Christian, but no more. There was a teacher who I knew was a secret believer. I knew he had a Bible. I went to the teacher and he read the Scripture to me; I prayed with him and accepted Jesus Christ. He gave me a Bible, which I still have."

This young man went on to tell me about what was happening on the campus: "Suddenly Bible studies appeared on the lawns, in public rooms, in classrooms. A professor of Philosophy brought out his Bible and said that from now on it would be his textbook. The writings of Marx, Lenin, and Che Guevera were replaced by Francis Schaeffer and Chuck Colson. When we had a celebration, a birthday or wedding reception, the featured entertainment was the 'Jesus film.'"

There are few things as exciting as sitting in a room and listening to Chinese young people, the "Flowers of the Revolution," as they confirm God's promise. "Though our house leaders have been arrested and imprisoned for illegal activity against the state, the Bible studies continue. This persecution is good for us. It is like a college examination, only we won't fail."

Today, at one end of the now famous Tiananmen Square, where a visitor can still see the blood stains of the massacre, hangs a larger-than-life, benign portrait of the Great Helmsman, another name for Mao. In gold, using the letters of the simplified language, are the words "SERVING THE PEOPLE."

Nearby is Mao's tomb. From a distance it looks like the Lincoln Memorial in Washington, D.C. Mao lies in state . . . very dead. Outside the exit, Chinese capitalists sell all kinds of Chinese souvenirs, everything except Mao's Little Red Book. At the opposite end of Tiananmen Square, facing Mao's declaration, is a McDonalds restaurant—and people world-wide know their motto: "Billions Served." Mao, a god in his own eyes, has been upstaged by Ronald McDonald, the clown.

This lesson is more spiritual than social. I spent a few years attempting to reach China, and I attended a few seminars on that subject. I heard some people say, "If only we could get Mao saved . . ." or, "Let's increase the power of our transmitters." I never heard the idea that God was using Mao to purify His Church set forth as a viable consideration. Now, I feel like one of Joseph's brothers. I am finally learning the lesson that though man may mean something for evil, God always uses it for good.

". . . we know that God causes all things to work together for good to those who love God, to those who are called according to his purpose."
—Paul

Lesson 2. *All things really do work together for good for those who love God.*

There are some Bible verses that we have heard so many times they have become little more than linguistic reflexes. However, we can know the Scriptures but still not "know" them.

How many times I have used the above verse as a bromide

rather than a tonic, spoken it by rote like a mathematical for-
mula, or used it to end a conversation in which I was losing inter-
est.

This was forcefully driven home to me on an early trip to
Beijing. I sat in a small, sparsely furnished flat, facing an elderly
woman. Her white hair and furrowed face were evidence of a life
of suffering, but the infectious smile and sparkling eyes spoke of
one who understood that the apostle Paul was right. Her voice was
soft-spoken, and her words were sometimes tinged with sadness,
sometimes with joy. They were so matter-of-factly intermingled
with Scripture, however, that it was difficult to tell when she was
quoting large portions of the Bible that she had memorized or
when she was simply describing her own experience:

"As I told you, I was led to the Lord by a missionary. I went to
medical school and became a surgeon. I worked in the hospital
here in Beijing, a hospital built by your Mr. Rockefeller. During
those terrible days of the Cultural Revolution many of my fellow
surgeons were taken into the courtyard of the hospital, where
many of the staff and patients had been assembled. They were
made to kneel and confess their crimes against Mao. Those that
could not think of any crimes made them up. After each session,
usually at least one doctor would be taken away, never to be seen
again. Many were executed; others were sent to work in the countryside and some went to prison.

"A fellow surgeon—another woman—and I knew that it
would happen to us one day, but we still were not prepared when,
one morning during surgery, the Red Guards came into the operating room and dragged us out into the courtyard. I found out
later our patient died on the operating table.

"They made us kneel on the ground, then hit and kicked us,
screaming at us to confess that we worked for a foreigner, Mr.
Rockefeller, and that he was putting money away for us in New

York. Of course it was a lie. We were missionary doctors. We kept only enough of our salary to live. The accusations and assault went on for hours until they got hungry or hoarse from their scream-ing. I can still hear the young man, not more than sixteen or sev-enteen, pulling me up by my surgical gown, his breath hot and foul, smelling of danger and acid, yelling, 'Parasite, Parasite!' Others joined in, and finally, he threw me to the ground and left. He was followed by his 'little soldiers.' One by one the hospital workers went back inside, knowing that one day it would be their turn—maybe tomorrow.

"Two young men and one young girl stayed behind and led us to a small room where they pronounced our sentence. The girl was especially angry with us because we would only quote Scriptures.

"We were sentenced to 'serve the people.' We had been 'para-sites' long enough, now we would 'use our hands to serve the peo-ple.' We were assigned to clean the hospital latrines. The latrines were long metal troughs, some ten or twenty feet long, with boards across them for seats. There was no water, only a large hole in the bottom of the trough at one end with a bucket underneath. Our job was to keep them clean 'for the people' from early morn-ing to late at night, seven days a week."

Again, with my usual spiritual perception, I fumbled for some words of sympathy, and finally, awkwardly attempting to empathize, "That must have been a terrible experience, trained surgeons using your hands to clean toilets."

Those hands, blue veins protruding through skin, now translucent with age, reached out and took my pampered hands, which had never been used for anything more radical than press-ing down a chrome lever to release the tank of bubble-blue water to flush away life's unmentionables. "Oh no!" she exclaimed with deep sincerity. "It was wonderful. We were given a bucket of water and a white rag. We kneeled down in front of the trough and tears would come as we began our devotions. People were sitting on the latrine, but we didn't mind. We wept when we saw the foul waste and smelled the stench, and we cried to the Lord, 'Oh Jesus, that is the way my heart used to be, full of waste, a stench to those around me and to You. But dear Jesus, You came and gave us Your Holy Spirit to make us clean.' We would pour water into the trough and pray, 'Thank You for giving us your Word.' Our rags became a symbol of His precious Word, and we would scrub and scrub, asking Jesus to purify our hearts as we were cleaning those latrines."

There was a strong squeeze of my hand, and her face was not so much smiling as it was glowing as she said, "And brother, we had the cleanest latrines in China because we wanted to have the cleanest hearts in China."

As the apostle Paul taught, "All things work together for good to them who love the Lord...."

". . . to this end also I wrote that I might put you to the test, whether you are obedient in all things." —Paul

Lesson 3.   *God's Word dictates our lifestyle.*

When I (David Wang) was a young pastor in Hong Kong, I remember preaching to about seventy young people from several house churches in a remote region of northwestern China. To start, I took about three hours to preach on the Lord's Prayer. The young people were squatting and sitting on the mud floor or leaning against the wall of the little hut. They listened and wrote down every word I spoke.

After I finished, the house church leader gave me some tea, saying, "Please have some tea, and then you can preach to us again." Now that was after three hours of solid preaching! I took my tea and preached for another four hours. All this time these young people took notes, echoing, "Amen, amen." Finally, I sat down, totally exhausted. The house church leader said, "Now let us sing." So they began to sing and I was shocked as I listened to their song. The first verse went something like this:

> Don't listen to sermons,
>   don't listen to sermons.
> We will not listen to sermons . . .

After almost seven hours of listening to sermons they were singing, "Don't listen to sermons," but they then clenched their fists and sang:

> We will live out the sermons!

". . . without faith it is impossible to please Him . . ." —*Paul*

Lesson 4.   Trust in God with your whole heart.

Without faith, without trusting, man cannot please God. Pastor Wang Mingdao represents the integrity of the Chinese Christian Church. He was a pillar of the Chinese Church and earned the nickname "The St. Paul of China."

He was arrested, persecuted, and imprisoned for about twenty-five years. It was only in 1980, at the age of 80, that he was finally released. Living in his little room in Shanghai, half blind, feeble, and suffering from a number of illnesses after so many years in labor camps and prison cells, he prided himself on being able to still sing in a good, loud voice. "Listen to me," he would say. "I can still sing hymns. And when I sing, the whole street and block can hear me." He was praising God for preserving his voice.

He believes that the Church in China is experiencing such frequent, magnificent and gloriously divine interventions because China's Church had no Bible, no church buildings, no missionaries, no Bible schools and no seminaries. "Perhaps it is because we had nothing. Therefore God had special mercy on us. He has given us the faith of a mustard seed, simple childlike trust in Him. The Chinese Christians just believe God and His Word. We believe that He is able and willing to do great things for us."

There is an elderly pastor who was imprisoned in a labor camp for many years. He was released in 1981, when his daughter applied for him to go to Hong Kong for a visit. After a short stay, he decided to return to China. He felt that the Christians in Hong Kong didn't need him, but the Christians in China did. When he described the difference between the churches in China and Hong Kong, he was not critical. Instead, he was matter-of-fact when he said, "I think the Hong Kong Christians know much about God, but the Christians in China know God."

"Love one another, just as I have loved you." —Jesus Christ

Lesson 5. *Christians must love one another.*

The Greek word for 'fellowship' is '*koinonia*. It is a very descriptive word. It means to open up your life and let your blood flow into another person's body while letting that person's blood flow into yours. This interflow of life is *koinonia*. The Western world seems to see 'fellowship' as 'fellows who are in the same ship.' That's good but not deep enough to capture the full meaning of the word 'koinonia.'

How do Chinese Christians fellowship, particularly when they are going through trials and tests?

Pastor Chen is an associate worker of Asian Outreach. He helps produce gospel radio broadcasts for China. Pastor Chen has been an itinerant evangelist, working in central China for almost thirty years, eighteen of which were spent in hard labor camps.

"I considered being transferred from one camp to another as a change of mission field," he said, "but the most wonderful thing was I could always be sure of beautiful Christian fellowship no matter which camp I was sent to."

From 1959 to 1962, Pastor Chen was imprisoned in a hard labor camp in Anhui province. It was during the so-called "natural disaster years." The whole of China suffered devastating famine, primarily because of the disastrous result of communization, which was only compounded by drought. Millions starved to death. In Pastor Chen's camp, everything was severely rationed. They had one meager meal a day.

"I remember our feast," he recalled. "It was Chinese New Year's Eve, and every one of us was given an egg. One egg a year—that was celebration, our feast of the New Year. The campmates hard-boiled their eggs and ate the whole thing, of course. They crushed the eggshell into powder and drank it down with water. That was for the calcium. Everyone was desperate."

However, instead of eating that once-a-year feast, the Christians gathered their eggs and took them to brothers and sisters who were sick and weak. He said, "We would urge them to eat the eggs because they needed more nourishment. We wanted them to get well and strong." Now that is true fellowship. It is by this kind of love that the world saw that they were Christians.

When Pastor Chen was finally released from the labor camp, the Chief and Deputy Chief, both hard-core atheistic Communists, came to the station to send him off. In front of each other they confessed, "After observing you Christians for many years, we are both convinced that your Jesus is real."

Notes:

1.   Jonathan Chao, Ph.D., *What the Beijing Massacre Means For the Future of China and The Gospel*, Chinese Church Research Center, Hong Kong.

16

MORE LESSONS

". . . make disciples of all the nations . . . teaching them to observe
all that I commanded you."
—Jesus Christ

Lesson 6.   The Great Commission must be taken seriously.

We all talk about the "Great Commission" of our Lord Jesus Christ, but in China's Church there is a seriousness about carrying it out in day-to-day life.

A Western missionary went to China for one of his many survey trips. He is head of his mission's work in China, and he speaks the language fluently. When the train he was riding in stopped over in a small town, a young hawker came into the carriage carrying candies, cakes and the like in a rattan basket. He went around selling his merchandise, then settled himself near the missionary. In his very broken English, he tried to strike up a conversation with the foreigner.

When the young hawker noticed that the passengers around them had gone, he pointed to himself and to the missionary as he said, "I am Christian. You Christian?"

The missionary could have easily switched the conversation into Chinese to make life a lot easier for this young fellow. But he was in a playful mood, so he coolly replied in English, "Yes, I am a Christian."

The young man was not totally satisfied with the answer. Perhaps he had learned that most Westerners think of themselves as Christians. So he pressed on, "Are you two-time born Christian?" Of course the missionary knew what he was trying to say. He wanted to find out what this young man was trying to get at, and find out more about his theology, so he asked the fellow to explain.

That young man tried so hard in English to make this white fellow understand the importance of being "born again" that he himself was turning red with excitement. Finally the missionary took pity on his predicament and told him that he spoke Chinese. The young man was then very happy that he could now explain more clearly that everyone must be a born-again Christian! The missionary was amazed, both at the young man's enthusiasm and his sense of urgency: "You must become two-time born Christian!"

At last, wishing to somehow end the conversation, he told the young hawker that he was a born-again Christian and further-more, a missionary. That didn't seem enough. The young man persisted, "Good! And how many people did you bring to Christ last month?" It seemed that nothing could stop the young man from talking about Jesus.

Later the missionary learned that this young man was for-merly a soldier in the People's Liberation Army. He had to leave that privileged class because he became a Christian—booted out by the People's Army but accepted into the Lord's Army.

After returning to his village, the young man joined a rapidly growing Christian fellowship. The other believers discovered that he had the gift of evangelism and personal witnessing, so they helped him obtain a license to sell on the trains. "They did this so I could meet strangers and tell them about Jesus," he told the missionary. "I love to tell everyone about Jesus. And we must work while we still have the opportunity, because Jesus is coming back soon!"

Often our evangelism in the West is too program-oriented. We depend on Evangelism Explosion Seminars to keep us going for awhile, and then we wait for the next specialist to come around with another program. If we are serious about the Commission from our Lord, we will grab every opportunity to talk about Jesus Christ, even when we are peddling goods on the streets, selling insurance, or directing a company. That young man typifies many new Christians I've met in China. They just cannot stop talking about their Lord.

". . . our struggle . . . is against the powers, against the world forces of this darkness, against the spiritual forces of wickedness . . ." —Paul

Lesson 7. *Recognize that we are involved in a spiritual war.*

The Christians in China have a crystal clear understanding that they are engaged in spiritual warfare. They know they are not fighting the government, nor are they fighting a system or ideology. They know they are wrestling . . . *against the rulers, against the powers, against the world forces of this darkness, against the spiritual forces of wickedness in the heavenly places."* (Ephesians 6:12)

In Shanghai the woman whose family went through much torture and suffering because they were Christians said, "Don't feel sorry for us. At least we are constantly reminded that we are in a spiritual war. We know for whom we are fighting. We know who the enemy is. And we are fighting. Perhaps we should pray for you Christians outside China. In your leisure, in your affluence, in your freedom, sometimes you no longer realize that you are in spiritual warfare."

". . . Pray on my behalf, that utterance may be given to me in the opening of my mouth." —Paul

Lesson 8.   *Pray for Christian workers.*

There were many times that this pastor in Hong Kong, while given the credit for a fast growing ministry, would be greatly humbled by faithful warriors who "simply pray."

When China first opened up after the Cultural Revolution, I (David Wang) visited Beijing. While there, I was introduced to an elderly woman who was bedridden and whose body was wracked with arthritis and pain. She could barely hold a pencil in her hand and, once she grasped it, she kept it there because it was too painful to release it.

"I can do nothing. Look at me—deformed, ugly, no one wants to be around me. I am useless. I can't take care of myself. My two daughters have to bathe me and dress me. I am worthless."

I listened for a short period of time and then felt I'd listened long enough to her complaining. I wanted to leave, but then she asked me about my family and ministry. I answered her, and she began her "woe is me" lament again. "It has been so long since I could sleep. The pain is there day and night. If ever I sleep more than a few minutes, the pain wakes me up and reminds me of how useless an old woman I am."

Discouraged and annoyed, I was glad when the visit was over. However, I could not forget her.

Eighteen years later I was back in Beijing, and found myself with a rare, free afternoon. I wondered if the "old complainer" still lived in the same place. Beijing had changed; modern hotels had replaced decrepit buildings, modern thoroughfares were blocked with buses and automobiles. But it was still Beijing. In many ways, nothing had changed.

I rented a bicycle, looked again at the address that I had kept all these years, and within twenty minutes, recognized one of the old streets. I soon found the alley; it looked the same as it did eighteen years before. Dismounting the bike I called out, asking if anyone was home. Soon, I found myself ushered into the same dimly lit room. There, lying on the bed, was the old woman, so badly deformed that I was nearly sick. From her fetal position, she smiled at me and held out her gnarled hand: "David Wang." She asked about my wife and children, by name, and then she began her litany of complaints: "Look at me. I am only more useless than I was when you saw me last. What a useless old creature. I cannot even open my Bible any more."

I answered her many questions, but the whining was all I really heard. *I don't know why I bicycled all the way over here just to hear you complain,* I thought—but didn't say what I was thinking.

Then she painfully tried to reach under her pillow. With hands that looked like bird claws, she managed to pull out a book. She motioned for me to pick it up.

Bending over, I took it and opened it. It was a diary of names. As I read the names, I recognized many of them—the names of Christian workers in China. Looking up from the book, I realized I wasn't hearing her complain anymore. She was saying, "I prayed for you, for your wife, for your children, for your ministry . . . every day. Every day I prayed for you." Yes, there it was: my name, written there eighteen years before. I gazed in awe at this "whiner" and realized that she was one of the reasons I had a ministry—and why God had miraculously intervened when I had bungled a responsibility, and why I'd often experienced being able to teach more than I actually knew.

"I prayed for you every day, sometimes harder than other times. Sometimes you would come to my mind while I was praying for someone else, and I would stop and pray for you."

I thought back to my ministry years: there was the time I should have been arrested . . . those two young women who insisted they go to Hainan . . . the opportunities that came . . . the miracles . . .

Humbled, I closed the book and reverently tucked it under her pillow again.

"I am a useless old lady." She picked up the refrain where she had left off. "I am no use to anyone. But I pray for you every day."

The words were the same eighteen years ago as they were when I first came into the house; the face was the same—but somehow—nothing was the same. What had first made me want to turn away now drew me. The contorted hands locked together in prayer were the hands of an angel, a ministering spirit.

As I rode the bicycle back to the hotel, I had to stop several times to wipe my eyes. I'm sure that it was the smog of Beijing that had gotten to me.

"Blessed are you when men revile you and persecute you and say all kinds of evil against you falsely on account of me." —Jesus Christ

Lesson 9. There is a cost to pay.

The grammatical tense of the word "persecute," as our Lord uses it in His beatitudes, implies that it is not a one-time occurrence; rather, it continues through life. If you are poor in spirit, then expect to be persecuted. If you are meek, then expect to be persecuted. It will be an everyday occurrence; you won't have to pray for it. Just live as Jesus lived and you will experience it.

Few people understand that as well as the Chinese Christians. Their history is laced with times of great difficulty. Tourists from around the world flock to see the Great Wall, a fortification stretching about 1,500 miles, from the Gulf of Chihil in the

Yellow Sea to the gate of central Asia. It is one of the greatest building enterprises ever undertaken, and the only object on our planet that astronauts can easily identify from outer space. Amidst the praise of such a spectacular feat, we forget that thousands of bodies are buried in the wall, covered up where they fell exhausted, workers fainted from heat or cold, starvation or disease. It was built three centuries before Christ warned of persecution and its blessedness, before the advent of dirt movers, Caterpillar tractors and labor unions.

We also marvel at the Grand Canal, built in 589 B.C. Twelve hundred miles long, and every clod of dirt removed by a Chinese laborer.

More contemporary is the Long March. It is the cornerstone of Maoist mythology. In 1934, the forces of Chiang Kai Shek surrounded Mao and his Communist army. The Communists split into two forces and headed north to establish the Communist capital of Yennan, 6,000 miles away. There were no trains, no buses, and in many cases, no shoes—6,000 miles through wild, mountainous swamps, snow, ice, and dirt. To add a little discouragement along the way, there were ten Nationalist armies stationed in the different provinces. Mao's forces crossed eighteen mountain ranges on foot, and twenty-four rivers (without benefit of rafts). They fought at least one action every day. In one instance, they had to cross a 300-foot long suspension bridge that was suspended on sixteen iron chains. There were machine guns positioned on the far side to discourage their crossing. But it was the only way to Yennan. Mao's troops slung their weapons on their back and they went across the bridge hand over hand. When one would fall into the river, a victim of machine gun fire, another would take his place. Finally, one soldier made it across the bridge and grenaded the machine gun nest.

Another bridge had been covered with paraffin. When Mao's troops started across, it was set on fire. It was the troops that put out the fire by running through the flames.

One hundred and thirty thousand soldiers began the march; 20,000 arrived at the caves of Yennan.

The Great Wall, The Long March—they did not just happen. They were inspired by, and became a reality through, the leadership of a person, an individual committed to a task. The soldiers were not rebels who would let others die for the cause; they were revolutionaries who would stand in harm's way and be one of the first to die. Some of them were good, some were bad, but they changed history.

One man cut from the same cloth was a schoolteacher in Indiana by the name of Mikhail Gusenberg, later to become Michael Borodin. He was also an underground courier between Russia and the United States for the Communist Party.

In 1923, Lenin sent him to China as an advisor to help reorganize the Kuomintang into a strong, disciplined and centralized party. His disciples were Sun Yat Sen, Chiang Kai Shek, and a young Vietnamese man by the name of Ho Chi Minh.

An American correspondent once interviewed Borodin. The content of that interview illustrates for us how a soldier in Christ's army needs to be totally committed to his cause if he is to be qualified to answer the call of the house church to "come and help us."

"They say, Mr. Borodin, that you are here to take over China. I am sure my paper would be interested to know if this is true, or if not, just why have you come?"

"That's easy," he replied. "If you say my colleagues and I plan to take over this country, the answer is no. But if you say we believe that our ideas will one day take it over, the answer is yes. China has suffered for hundreds of years. She wants help. She has asked for it, and we intend to give it. That is why I am here. Have you any objections?"

"No," I countered with an effort at nonchalance. "But do you have any notion of what you are taking on? I was born here and I know. How many people do you think live in this country?"

"About 500 million. Why?"

"Don't tell me you seriously mean to take over a fifth of the human race. In the first place, you are too few. You're only a handful with no knowledge of the land or the language. You'll never do it in a thousand years."

"Oh yes, we will," came the cool reply. "You forget young man that I am not here for my health, or I would not be working in the barbarous heat. I don't spend my time at the bars and races like the English and French. I am not interested in a career or a fortune like the Americans. I serve an ideology. And with an ideology, it is not numbers that count. It is dedication. You Americans would not understand that. I have lived many years in your country and I know what goes on. You concentrate on comfort and personal success. You had the chance, but you don't care. I'm interested in China. I am here to help her find something that will change things."

"Do you enjoy your work in China, Mr. Borodin?"

"Enjoy?" he echoed scornfully. A bourgeois question. It is not a matter of whether we enjoy our work here. The work is necessary. That is all that counts. It is, of course, far from the friends, the concerts and the theater that mean so much in Moscow. But long ago I made up my mind that Communism alone held an answer for the world, because Communism, unlike modern religion, insists on changing things. The Party decided I could help most in China. Therefore, I was glad to come. Nothing else matters. Does that answer your question?"

After a long silence, Borodin began murmuring, half to himself, "You know," he mused, "I used to read the New Testament.

Again and again I read it. It is the most wonderful story ever told. That man, Paul, he was a real revolutionary. I take my hat off to him." He made a symbolic gesture, with his long black hair falling momentarily over his face.

Another long silence.

Then suddenly Borodin whirled around, his face contorted with fury as he shook his fist in my face.

"But where do you find him today?" he shouted. "Answer me that, Mr. Roots. Where do you find him? Where? Where? Where?"[1]

The Long March left a wake of dead and dying, but it helped change a nation. That change continued with the Cultural Revolution, which set the stage for the Church of secret believers that paid the ultimate price. In the end, that change may affect more than a nation—it might, perhaps, reach an entire world.

In the end, when the crowns are ready for distribution, along with the Hudson Taylors and Jonathan Goforths, there will be a multitude of 'little people' rising from the dust of history to hear the words, "*Well done, thou good and faithful servant.*" God often uses what we consider insignificant to accomplish what he considers significant. Hudson Taylor's first recruits for missionary service in China were "a group who could quote the Bible, chapter and verse, but had little formal education. The seven men included, for example, a grocer, a cabinetmaker, a mechanic, and a printer. The eight women (all unmarried, as were the men) had worked as teachers or stenographers, or had lived as 'spinster daughters' within their families."[2]

A group of twenty missionaries were brought into a Chinese provincial governor's yamen to be ritualistically beheaded in his presence. Though their names are unknown to us, our Lord knows the name of each one. One of those "insignificant" missionaries wrote a note that was found after her death: "I was very restless and excited while there seemed a chance of life but God has taken away that feeling, and now I just pray for grace to meet the terrible end bravely." Another of that group wrote: "I am like the ox, ready for either—the plough or the altar."[3]

Such testimonies blend with the river of testimonies that one hears in China today. The message that often comes from the Church in the West is that as Christians, we can be happy, wealthy, and comfortable. Furthermore, we often think we have every right to expect a warm, welcoming, 'user-friendly' church, where our every need will be met. That message represents a heresy every bit as troublesome as any heresy being fought in China today.

". . . continue in the things you have learned and become convinced of, knowing from whom you have learned them." —Paul

We hope and pray that you are asking yourself, "What now?" Perhaps you already give money to send Bibles into China. Perhaps you've considered going to China as a tentmaker but you have responsibilities you cannot leave behind. Perhaps you privately yearn to be a part of a church that resembles the Church in China. How can you be involved, besides reading this book?

A good place to start is to be teachable. Be willing to be a learner that doesn't have all the answers—the neophyte, instead of the expert. Let what you know of China's house church disciple you. You'll be surprised how many of the problems faced by the Church in China are similar to those faced by your own church.

Here is a Church that has goals; they want to turn their country into a Christian nation that will help evangelize the world. Their goals should be our goals as well.

In order to fulfill that mandate, the Church in China exhorts all to be:

1. Students of the Bible.
2. People of daily prayer—(Actually praying, not just attending seminars on prayer).
3. Believing in and following the leading of the Holy Spirit.
4. Leading a holy life with Jesus Christ as Lord of their life.
5. Witnessing to the world through their daily lives, actions, vocations and home life.

Forget about persecution; it will come without an invitation. In fact, if you live in the West you may already be one of the most persecuted people in the world—only your persecution is cerebral instead of physical (but that's another book).

No one in China died for his or her faith in vain. Some died so that they could be a teacher to you. They suffered and died so that we might learn.

The lessons they learned are for us as well. Their culture may be different, but our Lord is the same—and His message is the same.

"By faith Abel offered to God a better sacrifice . . .
and through faith, though he is dead, he still speaks."
(Hebrews 11: 4)

Notes:

1. John McComb Roots, *Chou: An Informal Biography*, (N.Y.: Doubleday, 1978), pp.33-35.
2. Alvyn Austin, *Saving China*, (University of Toronto Press, 1986), p. 22.
3. Austin, p. 76

CONCLUSION

Over four decades have passed since the first events recorded in this story took their toll on the world's psyche. Many of those years have been distorted by historians' words, honed to fit their own pre-existing attitudes. Others are marred by mass graves, defoliated jungles, and strutting dictators.

Man records history in a feeble attempt to harness something that he neither created, controls, nor understands. However, we cannot—we must not—turn away, closing our eyes in an attempt to forget or ignore the people and events, the joy and the pain that make up life.

The flat on MacDonnell Road in Hong Kong that was mentioned in the introduction of this book, like the city over which it looked, has disappeared. It has since been replaced by a maze of high-rise office buildings, monuments to the babel of modern day materialism and the necessary high-tech language that dictates one's survival. They are poignant reminders that man and his artful intelligence in our modern times frightfully parallels his earlier brethren and the tower they constructed to reach the sky.

And what happened to the young Chinese kid on the first floor of 27 MacDonnell Road? He no longer walks through the maze of Hong Kong streets, wondering if all that his mother taught him about God, Heaven, and Jesus could really be true.

Now, as a pastor, he walks slowly, stooping over so as not to hit his head on a cave honed out of the side of a hill. He spends hours on a cold floor, feeding hungry minds with Words affirming that what he learned is indeed Truth.

The missionary who was on the fourth floor of that flat writes the conclusion to this book nearly thirty years later—far above the clouds, racing the sun to get back to the comforts of his little home and his wife in Corvallis, Oregon. Bone tired and a bit nauseated, he puts his fingers to the keyboard of the computer on his lap. He begins to type the historic words of a British journalist who, while looking out the window of his hotel in Shanghai in 1949, saw the flames of Mao's army advancing through the city and filed his last report from China:

"Tonight Shanghai is burning
    And I am dying too,
For there is no death more certain
    Than death inside of you.
Some men die of shrapnel,
    Some go down in flames,
But most men die, inch by inch,
    While playing little games."

He checks the words on the screen and saves them. Two beeps tell him it is finished. He then touches the "sleep" button, and the words disappear into a vortex, much like a lifetime does in eternity, becoming a small pinhead in the middle of a screen that goes dark.

He closes the lid of his computer, pushes his seat back, and turns off the overhead light. The plane is dark; only the flicker from a movie screen intrudes. Closing his eyes, he leans back and thinks about what has been involved in piercing the curtain that for so long separated China from the rest of the word. Though at times there seemed to be more persecution than progress, Jesus has continued to build his Church. Further, that Church is reaching out to influence the rest of the world. The devastation that Mao's regime caused the nation of China is in many ways like the devastation that swarms of locusts cause to fields.

He breathes a prayer: "Thank you, Lord, for this opportunity, and for returning some of the years that the locusts have eaten."

Epilogue

June 25, 2000. It was nearing the third anniversary of the return of Hong Kong to China. A group of friends had gathered in a private dining room in a popular Hong Kong seafood restaurant. The food was superb—when it comes to fresh seafood, Hong Kong is still the best. The diners—a couple of university professors, a civil service director, an architect, a television producer, the chief editor of the city's largest circulating newspaper, a legislator and me, a pastor—all knew each other well. The resultant conversation was uninhibited, intelligent, enlightening and at times, entertaining. The general consensus was that Hong Kong, China's first Special Administrative Region (SAR), needed help.

The editor revealed that he even wanted to write an editorial for July 1, the anniversary of the hand-over, to rally for a million signatures to petition Beijing to invite the British back to save Hong Kong. "We should pay whatever it costs to get the British back to run Hong Kong. We're in such a mess now!" he exclaimed.

Amidst the roaring laughter, the diners could not help but agree: Three years after the hand-over, under the "one country, two systems" and "Hong Kong people govern Hong Kong" policy, the former British colony was in its worst predicament.

The editor concluded his proposed editorial: "I shall end the appeal by crying, 'We need the British! We want the British! We must have the British! Will the Union Jack please come flying back?'"

There was more laughter but also some somber thought. On the surface, everything in Hong Kong seems to be the same. The city is still bustling, skyscrapers are still shooting up out of the ground, people are still busy making money, and the tourists are still pouring in. Deep inside though, Hong Kong has forever changed.

How? According to the dinner group, a number of subtle but core changes have taken place over the past two years: First, the government and Chief Executive—an "elected" governor from a Beijing-approved pool of candidates—seem to have set in their minds that pleasing Beijing is the supreme mandate. Second, cronyism and corruption, the thousand year old plagues of the Chinese imperial courts, are fast creeping into Hong Kong's governing structure. This has led to the deterioration of the once highly acclaimed civil service. The "less is better" governing philosophy of colonial Hong Kong is rapidly changing to a "more is better," China-like, central control way of thinking. It is squeezing a keenly competitive capitalistic society into the strait jacket of socialism. Consequently, instead of working to stay ahead as a world class city, Hong Kong is actually conforming to the Mainland China city mold.

As I listened to the conversation, my mind turned to a few significant dates over the last three years:

July 1, 1998

This marked the first anniversary of China's resumption of sovereignty over Hong Kong. It was a gloomy first year for the SAR, but not in the way pessimists had expected; the crisis had nothing to do with the issue of political freedom. Rather, it came in the form of the Asian economic meltdown just three months after the hand-over, and the city was caught totally off guard. The real estate market took a sharp nose-dive, and literally overnight, the city's economic bubble burst. Property is Hong Kong's only commodity and the market's downturn affected everything. The Pearl of the Orient was losing its luster.

In terms of the Church in Hong Kong, the July 1, 1997 hand-over had proved to be a great time management tool and deadline, sounding for Christians a long, loud signal to change, to adapt, to capture present opportunities, and to plan and prepare for the future. They were aware that they must no longer carry on "business as usual." As a result, Christians were motivated to make a high commitment to prayer and to foster new unity amongst the different churches and their leaders. Evangelism also took on an urgency, being conducted as if the return of the Lord was imminent, and Bible schools reported record numbers of student enrollments.

Now that the hand-over dust has settled though, Hong Kong seems to have lost its direction. It is searching for a new identity, new meaning and a new role as it tries to relate to a fast-changing China and the rest of the world. From a political standpoint Beijing has kept its promise to leave the SAR alone. This hands-off, "one country, two systems rule" is supposed to last for at least fifty years; Hong Kong is to be governed by the people of Hong Kong.

While the world (including Hong Kong) was wondering and worrying if China would actually comply with the policy, it has been, ironically, the Hong Kong government itself that has appeared reluctant to hold its own reins. When crises have actually arisen—for example, the collapse of the economy, or when the validity of the legal system and the right of abode (which led to fear of a potentially large influx of Chinese nationals flooding across Hong Kong's border) were being challenged—the local government proved inadequate. Civil servants, once touted the best in

Asia, are now ridiculed as the highest-paid but the least perform-ing.

Suicide rates in the SAR escalated to a record high, rising from 597 in 1997 to 882 in 1999. Unemployment, previously alien to Hong Kong, suddenly became an urgent and growing issue, threatening the stability of society. In 1997, the unemployment rate was 2.2 percent. By July 2000, it rose to a high of 5 percent. "Prosperity" and "stability," the two high-flying standards over the city during the 1997 hoopla, were quietly lowered. No one talks about them anymore.

With these economic and social woes, however, churches in Hong Kong are finding that people are more receptive to the gospel, which can now be found in newspapers, on the radio, in market places and on street corners. Without a doubt, there is an ever-increasing amount of sharing the Good News in the SAR, but other religions are active too. Local Buddhists, breaking away from their tradition of passivity, have conducted their own mas-sive celebration and prayer meetings and even youth rallies. The once super-materialistic city has become religious.

October 1, 1999

The world's most populous nation (1.3 billion) celebrates the 50th anniversary of Mao's revolution and the founding of the People's Republic of China. The occasion is marked with a parade through Tiananmen Square of high-tech military weapons and an aerial formation of fighter jets, bombers and helicopters. Multinational corporations search for new investment opportuni-ties and the central government applauds its country's own speedy transformation. Yet everywhere in China, despite all of the nation's progress, one hears talk of a spiritual vacuum, a meaninglessness to it all.

Although there have been actual Christmas celebrations in

Beijing in recent years, it cannot be denied that many Chinese people remain woefully ignorant of the Scriptures and of the basic truths of salvation. Cults and religious sects—both foreign and indigenous aberrations—are springing up like weeds and plaguing the Church. The crying need remains for basic, practical Bible teaching that is culturally adapted to the Mainland Chinese.

Probably the most well-known Chinese cult activity outside the country is Falun Gong, a strange mixture of Buddhism, Taoism, meditation and breathing exercises. There was a crackdown on the cult in 1999, in response to Falun Gong's surprise act of surrounding the central government's headquarters in Beijing, banning the group from practicing "evil thinking" and threatening social stability. At the same time, the central government also moved to monitor internet religious websites more vigilantly. Not only Falun Gong, which is organized primarily through e-mail, but all websites in China are technically illegal unless all content is approved by authorities.

Unfortunately, Christians in China have also suffered as a result of the Falun Gong crackdown. The definition of "cult" is becoming looser and broader, and local officials are erroneously thinking there is no difference between Christian house churches and the cults. Officially, the Communist government still considers groups that refuse to come under state control (e.g. unregistered house churches) to be a threat to society. President Jiang Zemin reiterated this stance in his National Day speech, vowing to crush unpatriotic, religious and separatist activity in ethnic minority regions.

Yet the house church movement has matured under persecution. "If we are sent to prison," house church leaders commonly say, "two things will happen: One, we will be able to start new ministries inside the prison. Two, on the outside, our younger leaders will assume a greater sense of responsibility and urgency."

In August 1998, seven leading house church leaders publicly appealed to the government for an end to persecution and to be recognized as a legitimate religious movement. The tone of their appeal was moderate with a willingness to open a dialogue with both the authorities and the Three Self Patriotic Movement. In a break from normal practice, the seven leaders allowed themselves to be photographed and their names to be published. The leaders said they were prepared to risk retaliation because government repression of house church activities was intensifying.

Not long afterwards, representatives from the major house church fellowships met to draft an unprecedented joint Confession of Faith that strongly reaffirmed evangelical Biblical faith and refuted various heresies. This aligned the theology and practice of China's house churches with mainstream evangelical Protestants worldwide.

In August 1999, more than thirty house church leaders, including some of the Confession of Faith signatories, were apprehended by National Security and local Public Security Bureau officers as they met for a prayer seminar in southwestern Henan. All except six were released after paying fines of up to RMB10,000 (US$1,200). The remaining six were sentenced to between one and three years of re-education through labor. They were charged with "using an evil cult to undermine the law."

One of those sentenced was Zhang Rongliang, affectionately known to many as Uncle Liang, the leader of one of the largest house church fellowships in China. In a surprising move, on February 3, 2000, Uncle Liang was released from prison on grounds of poor health. Uncle Liang has been a popular and highly active leader in Christian evangelism for nearly three decades. During the last twenty-six years he has been imprisoned several times for his Christian evangelistic activities, but this has not stopped him from sharing the gospel. Once again, he is committing his time to bringing about unity amongst the house churches in China, legalizing their position with the government, and overseeing the training of leadership in the house churches.

According to reports issued after the National Religious Affairs Bureau Conference in January 2000, "Religious affairs are now of deep concern to the leadership of the Chinese Communist Party. It is calling on provincial committees to urgently investigate and tackle the problems increasingly raised by the rapid growth of religion throughout China." At the conference a new document on religious policy, *"Concerning Some Policy Questions in Present Religious Work,"* was drawn by the Central Committee of the Chinese Communist Party and the State Council. This document calls for several things: (1) an overall tightening of religious control by ensuring that "patriotic" religious leaders act in a way to strengthen national unity and stability; (2) an increase in political appointees in the officially recognized Patriotic Catholic and Three Self Patriotic Churches, as well as the Patriotic Buddhists, Taoists and Muslims; and (3) heightened vigilance of foreign forces, which use the cloak of religion and the pretext of freedom of faith to interfere in, infiltrate and overturn China. The Communist Party also now insists that its members who attend religious activities must be disciplined and expelled if they refuse to "repent."

This conference confirmed that the growth of religious belief in China is viewed as a serious threat by the Party leadership, which is alarmed by the inroads made into its own ranks by religious faith, especially by Christianity. The measures taken to combat this are unimaginative and stereotypical—tighter control and increased ideological education.

During the conference, delegates were told the number of Protestants in China was 25 million. A leaked report from China's security organization, the Public Security Bureau put the total at 35 million.

Official spokesmen, such as China Christian Council Chairman Dr. Han Wenzao, have long denied the possibility that there are more than 15 million Christians in China. Three Self Patriotic Movement statistics claim there are only 13.3 million Protestants.

Foreign observers and house church leaders, however, claim the government is underestimating the number of Christians. House church membership is considered to be at least 50 million. Hong Kong based mission agencies estimate the total figure to be between 60 and 80 million.

Overall there is convincing proof of continuing persecution of Christians outside the official church in China, and this exposes the government propaganda that all Chinese citizens enjoy full religious freedom. Yet despite the persecution there are unprecedented numbers of people becoming Christians in China—current estimates are around 20,000 each day.

While for most of the past half century, the Church in China has been attacked by atheistic Communism, it now faces an even more forceful onslaught—atheistic materialism. Already, there are signs in many cities that young people have become enamored by the consumerism that has blighted the Church in the West. Urban China is rapidly catching up with the industrialized world. Shanghai, for example, is developing at such a fast rate that it has in some ways already surpassed Hong Kong—it has more efficient traffic, cleaner streets, taller buildings, richer cultural life and very eager consumers.

One evening, as I was visiting Shanghai, I took a walk with a few others. We were pushed left and right by the mass of people on the crowded street, which was glittering with neon lights even bigger and more dazzling than those seen on Hong Kong's famous "Golden Mile," Nathan Road. We stopped by a set of bronze, life-size statues that depicted a smiling family of husband, wife and child, loaded with shopping bags. "This is today's Shanghai," my host said, "tomorrow's China." He sounded a bit apprehensive, being an old-time Communist. "But changes are changes," he continued, "and no one can stop them."

December 20, 1999

The world did not pay much attention as Hong Kong's neighbor, Macau, became China's second SAR. The Portuguese, after more than 440 years of rule in Macau, were more than glad to get out. Beijing was not particularly excited to receive Macau back either. Unlike Hong Kong, Macau has never amounted to much—the city is notorious for its gambling, sex and violence.

Portugal began its rule of Macau in 1557. It was the port of entry for the infamous opium trade into China. It was also the place the very first Protestant missionaries, including Robert Morrison, gained their first footholds to learn the Chinese language and begin their Bible translation work. It was via Macau that Christianity saw a massive expansion throughout Asia.

In the last quarter of a century, however, Macau has been one of the least evangelized Chinese communities in the world. The church here is small and has tended to be divided and introspective, weakened by emigration and high turnover in leadership.

In the months prior to the handover though, the churches in Macau joined together and conducted many evangelistic events, and discipleship and leadership training meetings. Local ministries set a goal of visiting every household in the city before it returned to China, and more than 40,000 bibles were distributed. And on the night the tiny peninsula and two islands were actually being returned to China, with hundreds of business and political leaders gathered for a televised ceremony, Macau's Christians simultaneously held a ceremony dedicating their Church as "an evangelistic gift to China." Hundreds of people from different churches gathered at this joint rally to exalt the name of Jesus as their city was returned to the motherland. "We wish to be the modern day bearers of the Good News to China!" many Christians prayed that night.

Christians in Macau have been emboldened in thinking of their religious freedoms, particularly as they have seen how China has not interfered with churches in Hong Kong since its return. They want to build positive relationships with China's leaders to show that Christians and the government can work in harmony. It's been a long time coming, but the Christians in Macau are ready to serve their brothers and sisters in China.

March 18, 2000

The most recent presidential election in Taiwan sent a clear, strong message to the Mainland—"Stop telling us what to do! Stop bullying! Stop interfering with our internal affairs!" In electing Chen Shui-Bian, the people of Taiwan also said they are fed up with the corruption of the Kuomintang (Nationalist Party), which has retained power on the island for half a century.

Ultimately, the election result should mean better relations between Taiwan and China. Taiwan's Nationalist Party and the Mainland's Communist Party have opposed each other for more than fifty years. Chen's Democratic Progressive Party has a relatively clean slate with Beijing and can conduct affairs without old hatreds poisoning the atmosphere.

Taiwan's Christians overwhelmingly supported Chen in his election victory over former President Lee Teng-hui, who is a professed Christian. Chen does not claim to be a Christian himself, but his clean lifestyle, opposition to government corruption, and work to outlaw prostitution and to crack down on organized crime reflect a commitment to Christian ideals. With his election, the Mainland Communist government is more likely to be afraid of the influence of Christians. China's leaders fear that a democratic movement could emerge from the Church, similar to that of Poland in the late 1980s, and could topple the Chinese government. It is unlikely, however, that those fears will result in a backlash against Mainland churches because the Communists were embarrassed by the election results and will be keen to put on a better face to the outside world.

Local Christians have viewed the massive earthquake in Taiwan in September 1999 as a wake up call. Taiwan is a spiritual key to bringing revival to the Mainland; as a local businessman commented, "The earthquake was like the reminder Jonah received when he was running away from the mandate of God and trying to enjoy his good life. This is a critical moment for us Taiwanese, as we prepare to rebuild both physically and spiritually."

Christians on the island want to keep relations with the Mainland constructive so they can continue to visit and help strengthen the churches there. Taiwanese Christians believe God has called them to reach out to the 1.3 billion members of their "flesh and blood" across the strait with His love.

But the greatest force spreading His love is still found in China—the house church. These Christians are now preparing their workers to be sent out to every province in the country as "missionaries" to preach the Good News. In April 2000, one house church fellowship saw the graduation of 2,100 workers from a Hong Kong-originated correspondence theological training course. The one-year course was completed in less than six months. Another 1,600 would have graduated if their leaders had had enough time to grade their exams!

"We are now putting feet to the vision 'Back to Jerusalem,'" a keen second level leader of the largest house church movement in China told us. She assumed much of the responsibility of consolidating the thousands of house churches, scattered across the nation, when the six top-level leaders were arrested. "We are still convinced that the Chinese Church must bring the gospel back to Jerusalem, thus completing the 'Gospel Circle,' fulfilling the prophecy of our Lord, that His Gospel must be preached around the world; then the end shall come." Since the rise of indigenous leadership of the Chinese Church, such as Watchman Nee and Wang Mingdao in the late 30s, China's Christians have always accepted the challenge to bring the gospel back to Jerusalem.

The aim of the house church movement is simple: To bring the gospel into every one of China's 2,700 counties within the first decade of the new millennium and, at the same time, send their own "beautiful feet" teams to neighboring countries.

One of the most important criteria for joining those "beautiful feet" teams is a willingness to lay down one's own life. According to a key house church leader, "Our brothers and sisters are learning and memorizing the Word of God; they are also learning to pray for the sick and cast out evil spirits. Thousands have enrolled in the correspondence theological foundation course, but the most important thing is still to have a commitment to the Lord of the harvest, to be willing to become the kernel of wheat that is willing to drop to the ground and die, bearing fruit 30-, 60-, and even 100-fold."

While the world may be marveling at the size of China's population and the progress of its modernization in recent years, perhaps we should be looking beyond the physical surface, to what we can be learning from their church, and its coming influence in this age.

The Voice of the Martyrs
Serving the persecuted church since 1967

The Voice of the Martyrs is a nonprofit, interdenominational organization dedicated to assisting the persecuted church worldwide. VOM was founded over 30 years ago by Pastor Richard Wurmbrand, who was imprisoned in Communist Romania for fourteen years for his faith in Jesus Christ. His wife, Sabina, was imprisoned for three years. The Voice of the Martyrs works with a network of missions around the world.

VOM publishes a free monthly newsletter giving updates on the persecuted church and suggesting ways to help. To subscribe, call or write:

The Voice of the Martyrs
P.O. Box 443
Bartlesville, OK 74005
(800)747-0085
e-mail address: thevoice@vom-usa.org
Web site: www.persecution.com

Resources from The Voice of the Martyrs
China's Unreached Cities - $10.00
Paul Hattaway

Researcher and author Paul Hattaway examines the spiritual condition of 52 of the least evangelized cities in China today. Many Christians around the world know of the revival occurring in parts of eastern China, but few are aware that hundreds of millions of city-dwellers in China have never heard of Jesus Christ. Jim Nickel, president of the Institute of Chinese Studies, explains, "Christians comprise less than one percent of the population in most cities in China. Reaching them with the gospel of Jesus Christ is a daunting task, but it must be done." (Paperback, 124 pp.)

Eyes of the Tailless Animals - $10.00
Soon Ok Lee

"At the moment the officer announced my release in front of the prisoners, the eyes of all 6,000 'tailless animals' stared at me. Their eyes were pleading, 'When you get out of prison, be a witness for us.'" On October 26, 1986, Soon Ok Lee was enjoying a peaceful morning at work in Communist North Korea when she was summoned outside. She did not return to her family that night. Instead, she was taken to prison where she endured six years of inhumane treatment for refusing to satisfy the greed of a government officer. Witnessing the executions of Christians in prison, Soon Ok Lee could not understand why they stubbornly refused to yield to the government's demands to deny Christ. She later came to understand after escaping to South Korea where she found the Lord.

Juche: A Christian Study of North Korea's State Religion - $15.00
Thomas J. Belke

Take a journey into North Korea to view what is possibly the most rigidly controlling, godless religious system on the planet—*Juche.* Through unchallengeable totalitarian power, North Korea's ruling elite enforces *Juche* ideology in every aspect of the culture. Man is proclaimed God in a nation whose government has officially decided against Christianity for all of its citizens. The majority of North Koreans today have never heard the name of Jesus. This book is a major resource for study and prayer for exploring the various aspects of Juche, including its origins, central teachings, spiritual dimension, and holy sites, as well as a biblical view of North Korea's future. (Paperback, 418 pp.)

Tortured for Christ - $6.00
Pastor Richard Wurmbrand
This dramatic testimony shocked the Western world. After spending years in underground prison cells and solitary confinement, enduring inhumane tortures, Richard and Sabina Wurmbrand emerged with the testimony of today's Christian martyrs. The new 30th Anniversary Edition features photos, testimonies from Christian leaders, and an update on the work of The Voice of the Martyrs. (Paperback, 176 pp.)

In the Face of Surrender - $12.00
Pastor Richard Wurmbrand
This book contains over 200 true stories of ordinary people—sometimes sinful, sometimes saintly, often frightened, yet displaying great courage—some who failed, many who overcame in the face of surrender. No one is more qualified to tell these touching, faith-challenging stories than Richard Wurmbrand, who spent fourteen years in Communist Romania's prisons. As you read these stories, you will see the love and strength of Jesus Christ displayed through everyday lives of people who are surrendered to Him. Seeing Christ do the "impossible" through them will help you see that He can make all things possible for you as well. You will want to love and serve the Lord with a greater passion as you read of a depth of love and commitment rarely found in the free world. (Paperback, 347 pp.)

Between Two Tigers - $8.00
Compiled by Tom White
From forbidden baptisms and secret meetings to imprisonments, Christians in Vietnam pay a great price for their faith in Christ. Caught between Communist police and tribal religions, their many victories are evidence of God's faithfulness. *Between Two Tigers* is a collection of testimonies from today's persecuted Christians in Vietnam. (Paperback, 192 pp.)

The Triumphant Church - $4.00

Compiled by Voice of the Martyrs

A three-part study guide on suffering and persecution from the writings of Richard Wurmbrand, John Piper, and Milton Martin. An excellent tool for Bible studies, sermons, and understanding the persecuted church around the world.

> **Richard Wurmbrand** provides a forward look at the Church in the free world, which may someday be faced with the same challenges as believers in restricted nations globally: obey God or man.

> **Rev. John Piper** writes, "The deep things of life in God are discovered in suffering." From his book *Desiring God*, Piper articulates a challenging theology of suffering with such hope-filled insights as how Christians "complete" the afflictions of Christ through our own suffering (Colossians 1:24).

> **Milton Martin** introduces more than a dozen outlines for study and presentation on suffering and persecution through such themes as "Turning Trials into Triumph," "The Part of Suffering in the Life of the Believer," and hundreds of Scripture references. (Spiral bound, 112 pp.)

Videos by The Voice of the Martyrs

The Martyrs Cry - $15.00

Thirteen Sudanese boys are captured by the Islamic Army. Only nine survive to tell their dramatic story.

Rikka, an Indonesian teenage Christian, had a piece of broken glass forced against her stomach as she was told to deny Christ.

Ruth, a Vietnamese Hmong Christian, has witnessed so much persecution she no longer fears what the authorities can do to her. She is willing to die for Christ.

They live in different parts of the world and have grown up in different cultures, but they share one thing in common. They are more than conquerors in some of the worst persecution known to man for their faith in Jesus Christ. Join our brothers and sisters in Sudan, Southeast Asia, and Indonesia as they testify to the sufferings they have endured and how their faith allowed them to hold fast to the Rock of Salvation. Filmed on location and hosted by CNN's David Goodnow, this video brings you face to face with your persecuted family. (Approximately 27 minutes)

Faith Under Fire - $15.00

Faith Under Fire brings to life interviews with Christians who face persecution head-on. You will meet Zahid, once a persecutor of Christians until God gave him a "road to Damascus" experience and allowed his faith to grow under persecution in his Muslim homeland. You will visit a Chinese pastor's home and witness the "strike-hard" policy the Christians now face. And you will gain insight from the plight of Linh Dao, a Vietnamese teenager dealing with the arrest and imprisonment of her father for his work in the underground church. *Faith Under Fire* will challenge you to ask the question, "Is my faith ready to hold up under fire?" Don't miss the chance to be inspired by stories from another part of the Body of Christ. (30 minutes)

China: More Persecution, More Growing - $10.00

Pastor Samuel Lamb welcomes you to a worship service in his house church in Guangzhou, China. No stranger to the suffering of the persecuted church, this believer has spent over twenty years in prison and faces new imprisonment at any time. Undeterred, he continues to preach the saving message of Jesus Christ. Viewers will hear Lamb's stirring message as he challenges and encourages his brothers and sisters in the West, and learn about VOM work in China. (26 minutes)

Leaping China's Great Wall - $10.00

Come with us on a journey to the house churches of China. For decades, faithful Christians in China have defied their Communist government to meet secretly to worship God and proclaim the gospel. This video is a rare opportunity to meet Chinese Christians in their homes, share their sufferings, and rejoice in their victories. Leap over China's Great Wall and fellowship with these courageous believers. (30 minutes)

The Voice of the Martyrs has available many other books, videos, brochures, and other products to help you learn more about the persecuted church. In the U.S., to request a resource catalog, order materials, or receive our free monthly newsletter, call (800)747-0085 or write to:

The Voice of the Martyrs
P.O. Box 443
Bartlesville, OK 74005-0443

If you are in Canada, Australia, England, or New Zealand, contact:

The Voice of the Martyrs
P.O. Box 117
Port Credit
Mississauga, Ontario L5G 4L5
Canada

Release International
P.O. Box 19
Bromley BR2 9TZ
England

The Voice of the Martyrs
P.O. Box 598
Penrith NSW 2751
Australia

The Voice of the Martyrs
P.O. Box 69-158
Glendene, Auckland 1230
New Zealand